# THE ULSTER QUESTION
## 1603–1973

# The Ulster Question
# 1603—1973

T. W. MOODY

THE MERCIER PRESS
DUBLIN and CORK

THE MERCIER PRESS
4 BRIDGE STREET, CORK
25 LOWER ABBEY STREET, DUBLIN

First published 1974
Third edition 1978

ISBN 0 85342 399 7

PRINTED IN THE REPUBLIC OF IRELAND BY
THE LEINSTER LEADER LTD.,
NAAS, CO. KILDARE.

# CONTENTS

## MAPS

# PREFACE

The following is a revised and extended version of a paper delivered at St Patrick's College, Dublin, on 30 July 1973, in a course on the teaching of history in Great Britain and Ireland. The course, which had special reference to problems of prejudice and bias, was organised by the Department of Education of the Republic of Ireland in cooperation with the British Department of Education and Science, and was attended mainly by teachers from secondary schools in Ireland and Britain in roughly equal numbers.

The paper as delivered is broadly represented by parts I-VII below. Parts VIII and IX were mostly written in August, but take no account of events subsequent to July. The essay as a whole, together with a select bibliography and appendices, is published in the hope that it may contribute to understanding of the Northern Ireland problem.

As this goes to press the hopes raised by the elections to the new assembly have been in part realised. To the accompaniment of denunciations by the 'loyalists' on the one hand and by the Provisional I.R.A. on the other, the assembly has held its first sittings and set about its work; and despite the hostility of the 'loyalist coalition'—Mr Craig's Vanguard Party, Mr Paisley's Democratic Unionist Party, and the unpledged unionists led by Mr Harry West—agreement has at last been reached (22 November) between the official unionists, the Alliance Party, and the S.D.L.P. to form an executive under the headship of Mr Faulkner. The members of this executive-designate have entered into tripartite talks at Sunningdale, Berkshire, with representatives of the British government and of the government of the Irish Republic, and agreement has been reached (9 December) on the establishment of a council of Ireland and of common arrangements for the preservation of law and order throughout the island. The governments of the Irish Republic and of Britain have declared that the constitutional status of Northern Ireland may be changed only with the consent of a majority of the people of Northern Ireland, and the British government has declared that a decision thus taken by the people of Northern Ireland to unite with the Republic will have its support. These declarations are to be registered with the United Nations as international documents.[1]

The violence and the killings continue, and the British army remains in Northern Ireland. But after five anguished years there is an unprecedented change in the northern situation: a government is to take office on 1 January 1974 in which the elected representatives of the minority will share power with those of the majority, a government committed to restoring peace and promoting social justice and human welfare with the assurance of cooperation and support from the governments of the Irish Republic and of Britain. For this new departure a large share of the credit must go to Mr Whitelaw who, his mission accomplished, has resigned his post as secretary of state for Northern Ireland to become minister for employment in Britain (3 December).

All the parties in the northern conflict are in a sense prisoners of their past. Immense efforts are now being made on many levels to end that imprisonment. One means of liberation lies in seeking to understand the present situation in terms of its antecedents. That is what this essay seeks to do.

T. W. Moody

Trinity College, Dublin
9 December 1973

---

[1]The text of the Sunningdale communiqué is given below, pp 106-11.

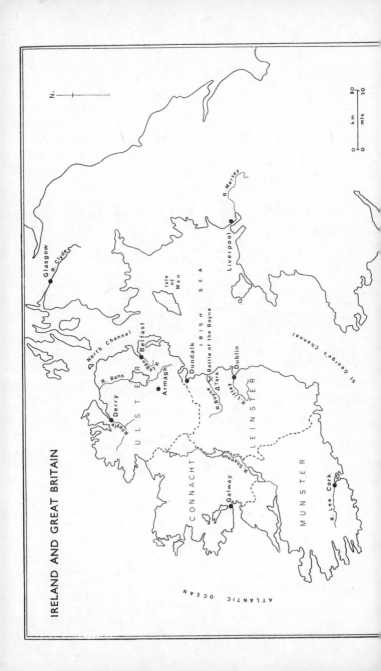

IRELAND AND GREAT BRITAIN

N

km 0        50    80
mls 0   50

Glasgow
R. Clyde

R. Mersey

Liverpool

North Channel

Isle
of
Man

IRISH SEA

Belfast
R. Lagan
R. Bann
Armagh

ULSTER

Derry
R. Foyle

Dundalk
Battle of the Boyne
R. Boyne
△ Tara
R. Liffey
Dublin

LEINSTER

St George's Channel

CONNACHT

R. Shannon

Galway

MUNSTER

R. Lee
Cork

ATLANTIC OCEAN

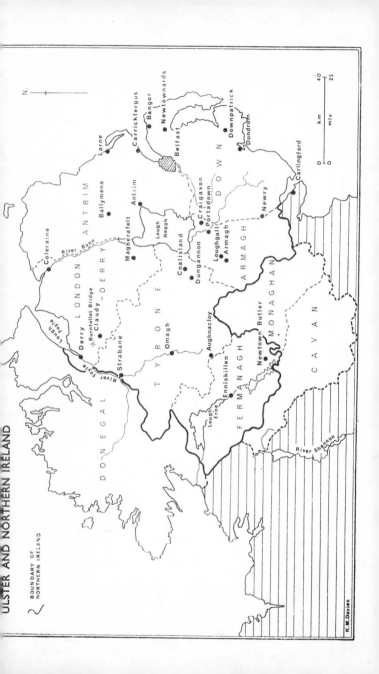

ULSTER AND NORTHERN IRELAND

BOUNDARY OF
NORTHERN IRELAND

N.

DONEGAL

LONDON-DERRY

Coleraine
River Bann
Magherafelt
Derry
Burntollet Bridge
Claudy
Strabane
River Foyle
Lough Foyle

ANTRIM

Larne
Carrickfergus
Bangor
Newtownards
Belfast
Ballymena
Antrim
Lough Neagh

TYRONE

Omagh
Coalisland
Dungannon
Aughnacloy

ARMAGH

Loughgall
Armagh
Craigavon
Portadown
Newry
Carlingford
DOWN
Downpatrick
Dundrum

FERMANAGH

Enniskillen
Lough Erne
Newtown Butler

MONAGHAN

CAVAN

River Shannon

km
0        40
mls
0        25

K.M.Davies

# I

## GAELIC ULSTER

The area broadly represented by the six counties of the
present Northern Ireland and three northern counties of
the Republic—Donegal, Monaghan and Cavan—has had
a distinctive identity from the earliest times. This has in
part been the product of geography. Till the seventeenth
century the belt of country stretching from Donegal Bay
to Dundalk and lying within the present counties of
Fermanagh, Monaghan, Armagh, Leitrim, Cavan and
Louth formed a strong natural barrier of interlacing hills,
lakes, rivers, forests, bogs and swamps; and while Ulster
was thus highly defensible against the south, it paradoxically offered at Larne and Belfast Lough the easiest gateway
into Ireland from the neighbouring island. Then too,
Ulster geographically resembles Ireland in miniature, with
Lough Neagh and the Bann river system corresponding
with the Shannon basin. These conditions, though greatly
modified since the early seventeenth century, have continued to exert an influence on the culture and outlook
of the Ulster population.

The Ulster shaped by geography only received its
modern definition as nine counties constituting one of the
four provinces of Ireland at the opening of the seventeenth century, but it had already had a political identity
for at least sixteen centuries, during which it had played
a prominent part in Irish history. It derived its name from
that of an ancient ruling aristocracy (the Ulaid) whose
centre of power was the great fort of Navan (Emain
Macha), near Armagh. This Ulster was inhabited by a
rural people, whose social and political structure was
based on family groups and local lordships, whose
economy was mainly pastoral, and whose principal wealth
was cattle. It was the setting of the most famous of the
heroic tales of ancient Ireland—the epic of King Conor
MacNessa and his Red Branch knights, of Deirdre and the
sons of Uisneach, of King Ailill and Queen Maev of
Connacht, and, above all, of Cúchulainn, mirror of all
the manly virtues of the pagan Gael. The Navan king-

dom was overthrown in the fifth century by a half-legendary prince of Connacht, known as Niall of the Nine Hostages, who seems to have wielded supremacy over all Ireland as high-king at Tara. He drove the Ulaid east of the Bann, and annexed the southern layers of the older Ulster to Connacht and Meath. His descendants, known as the northern Uí Néill, established kingdoms in the Ulster west of the Bann, of which Aileach, so called from the great fort of that name near Derry, became the most powerful. They extended their authority over most of Ulster west of the Bann, and from the fifth to the tenth century the high-kingship was monopolised by them and by their relatives, the southern Uí Néill, kings of Tara. East of the Bann the Ulaid established themselves as rulers of the modern Antrim and Down. A sub-kingdom in north-east Antrim, called Dál Riada, expanded (c. 500) across the narrow North Channel into Scotland in what is now Argyllshire, where many Ulstermen had already settled. This Irish outcrop became the nucleus of the later kingdom of Scotland and, incidentally, the source of its name; for the Irish were then known to the outside world as Scots.

The conversion of Ireland to Christianity in the fifth century, which had so profound an effect on Gaelic civilisation, gave Ulster a new distinction: for St Patrick, whose missionary career is more closely identified with Ulster than with any other province, established the capital of his church at Armagh, near the ancient pagan capital of Navan. In the golden age of Irish learning (sixth-eighth century), Ulster had its share of the great monastic schools, such as Armagh, Derry, Bangor and Moville (on Strangford Lough), that were famous throughout Christendom, and produced that most militant and athletic of Irish saints, Columcille of Derry (521-97), the pioneer of Christianity to the Picts of Scotland and the forerunner of a flood of Irish missionaries overseas, of whom the greatest, St Columbanus (d. 615), was educated at Bangor.

In the ninth and tenth centuries, kings of Aileach were in the front line of Irish resistance to the Norse invaders. By the middle of the twelfth century the ruling king, MacLochlainn, had won supremacy over nearly the whole of what had been the ancient province. But this was the peak point of Uí Néill power. Aileach became disrupted by dynastic conflict at the very time that the Irish political structure as a whole was being shattered by the invading

Normans. Two new states emerged: Tír Conaill (roughly the present county of Donegal), ruled by O'Donnell, and Tír Eóghain (covering the greater part of modern Tyrone, Londonderry and Armagh), ruled by O'Neill. The O'Neills, as the senior branch of the northern Uí Néill, claimed supremacy over all Ulster, a claim that the O'Donnells, also Uí Néill, strenuously resisted, so that the rivalry between them became a settled feature of Ulster politics. Nevertheless Tír Eóghain and Tír Conaill together exerted a determining influence on Ulster history for nearly four centuries. It was their resistance that halted the Norman invasion of the north at the line of the Bann. John de Courcy and his successors, from 1177 onwards, did indeed plant Norman colonies around the castles that they built at strategic points from Carlingford to Coleraine—a conquest to which the great strongholds of Carrickfergus and Dundrum still so impressively bear witness. But they failed in their efforts to found permanent settlements west of the Bann. In the fourteenth century, a branch of the O'Neills overran Antrim and Down and created the lordship of Clann Aedha Bhuidhe (Clandeboye). During the fifteenth century MacDonnells from the Western Isles of Scotland planted themselves strongly in the Glens of Antrim, while the old Norman colonies either became absorbed or were penned into a few coastal pockets—mainly Carrickfergus, the Ards and Lecale.

The Normans established English authority and English culture in Ireland but their conquest was never completed. The total conquest of the island, the work of the Tudor rulers of England in the sixteenth century, was the more embittered because the religious changes constituting the English reformation were introduced into Ireland as part of the Tudor policy of anglicisation. The protestant episcopal church established by law was the church of the new English conquerors, while the mass of Irishmen, though their church was proscribed, remained invincibly catholic. So the cause of Gaelic independence became linked with the cause of catholicism in Europe, and England was faced by the new peril of a Spanish attack upon her through Ireland. In this decisive conflict, Ulster was the heart of the Gaelic and catholic resistance, and Hugh O'Neill, earl of Tyrone, who came near to achieving a united Gaelic front in alliance with Spain, proved the most dangerous antagonist the English had ever encountered in Ireland. Queen Elizabeth had to exert all her strength before O'Neill and his confederates finally acknowledged defeat in 1603.

## II

## THE BRITISH COLONY

The submission of Hugh O'Neill marked the end of an era for Ulster and for Ireland. The conquest of Ireland that the Normans had begun in the twelfth century was for the first time complete: English law and government were now extended into every part of the island, and all that remained of the Gaelic states-system collapsed with the ruin of a dynasty that had spanned eleven centuries of Ulster history. Ulster, so long the citadel of Gaelic independence, and the most formidable danger to English power in Ireland, was now marked out as an area to be made safe for English authority and the English interest in Ireland once and for all. In Ulster Gaelic society had been least affected by English influences, and its characteristic virtues and vices were most fully displayed: a passion for local independence combined wth the idea of provincial kingship and a kingship of all Ireland; aristocracy tempered by informality and good-nature; the immense prestige of tradition and family ties in conflict with personal vanity and ambition; inordinate pride of ancestry and preoccupation with ancient feuds; delight in traditional story-telling, poetry and music; veneration for learning and religion; indifference to material improvement; absorption in abstractions to the neglect of concrete realities. The English regarded this archaic society as incurably diseased and in need of major surgical treatment. The replacement of Irish 'barbarism and superstition' by English 'civility and religion' was now to be undertaken as an integral part of the process of transforming Ulster into a stronghold of English authority. All this was to be achieved by a large-scale importation of protestant colonists from England and Scotland, which had just been united as Great Britain under the common monarchy of James I.

The foundations of the British colony that gave a new character to Ulster were laid in the early seventeenth century. The movement of colonisation began in Antrim and Down; and there, as in Monaghan, it continued to be the work of private adventurers, with official encouragement. But in the other six counties, Donegal, Londonderry, Tyrone, Fermanagh, Armagh and Cavan, it was initiated, organised and supervised directly by the government. There the intention was to clear out the native Irish completely from certain areas in each county, to segregate them in certain other areas reserved for them in each county, and to replace them with communities of English and Scottish colonists that would include all social classes. Now this central feature of the Ulster plantation scheme was never entirely realised: the Irish were too hard to displace, the colonists too glad to find tenants on the spot. There was never, in fact, any general removal of Irish from the lands assigned to colonists. But the plantation none the less meant a social revolution in Ulster, a clean sweep of all the traditional property-rights of the occupying Irish. Only a small number of Irishmen were continued as landowners under the scheme, and the whole area thus owned was only a small fraction of what was granted to the newcomers. The great mass of Ulster Irish remained on their former lands, but degraded to the status of tenants-at-will. As they became increasingly impoverished, economic pressure tended to drive them out of the more fertile and into the worst lands, where their descendants are still to be found.

The colonists, though for long outnumbered by the Irish, did gradually strike root; and a new and more dynamic society arose, based on their manor-houses, villages and towns. The most notable of these towns was Derry, re-named Londonderry in honour of the city of London through whose reluctant participation the entire county of Londonderry was ' planted '.[1] Derry, incorporated as a city, rebuilt on a formal and symmetrical plan and

[1]Though the official name of the city, as of the county associated with it, has been Londonderry since 1613, the ancient Irish name of the place, Derry, has continued to be used by most people locally and throughout Ireland; and though some unionists use Londonderry on principle, it is, on balance, I believe, less emotive to use Derry. In Orange tradition it is Derry's walls (not Londonderry's) that are the symbol of 'no surrender'. On the other hand there is much to be said for using Londonderry to describe the county, an area that had never been known as Derry or by any one Irish name before the city of London's connection with it.

5

surrounded by strong walls, became a citadel and symbol of the new regime in Ulster. In 1649 and in 1689, during the two most turbulent eras of the seventeenth century, when English power in Ireland was most dangerously threatened, Derry was twice besieged by resurgent Irish and twice maintained a successful resistance, on the second occasion withstanding an epic siege of over one hundred days. Numerically, the colony succeeded best in Antrim and Down, where it was not government-sponsored, and was least successful in Donegal, Cavan and Monaghan, of which the two former were 'planted' counties; in the four remaining counties, it was more successful in Londonderry and Armagh than in Tyrone and Fermanagh. Though, despite some intermixture, the colonial and the native elements remained distinct, they interacted powerfully upon each other. Thus, for example, the Irish language was superseded, wherever the colonists became entrenched, by an English that was deeply influenced by the native tongue. Again the fact that the colonists were no mere landowning superstructure but comprised real communities favoured a more healthy relationship between landlord and tenant than was to be the general rule in Ireland; the resulting 'Ulster custom' became, in the long run a boon to the supplanted as well as to their supplanters. On the other hand it has to be recognised that the colony was established in an atmosphere of ferocious hatred and bitterness. The occasion for the plantation scheme had been the flight and the alleged treason, in 1607, of the earls of Tyrone and Tyrconnell and other Irish chiefs who, though pardoned in 1603, had been unable to settle down under the new regime in Ulster. In this crisis the mass of the native population were assured by the government that their property rights would be respected if they kept the peace. They did keep the peace and no general rising followed the 'flight'. But the government's promise was blatantly ignored in the greatest single act of confiscation that had ever been inflicted by the English on the Irish; and the mass of the Ulster Irish could regard the plantation in no other light than as a monstrous injustice, made the more insufferable because cloaked with the forms of legality. The reaction of the most spirited and reckless of the dispossessed was to 'stand on their keeping'—to become outlaws (known as 'swordmen' or 'wood-kernes' in the early seventeenth century and as 'tories' from about 1650)—and to seek revenge on their supplanters by sporadic outrage and terrorism. This in turn provoked no less ferocious counter-activities from the colonists and induced in them a siege mentality that became one of their dominant characteristics.

Viewed as a whole the Ulster colony fulfilled the purposes of its authors better than any other British colony in Ireland. It resisted absorption and chronic guerilla attack, never lost confidence in itself, and contributed decisively to the defeat of catholic Ireland in the two great concerted efforts—of 1641 and 1689—to undo the English conquest. Fundamentally this was due to qualities in the Ulster colonists, above all to those who came from Scotland. The nearness of Scotland to Ulster and their mutual accessibility had from the earliest times ensured close connections between them. Before 1603, the Scots who had settled in Ulster, notably the MacDonnells of the Glens, were just as Gaelic as the Ulstermen who had migrated to Argyll centuries earlier, and therefore they had not disturbed the cultural balance of Ulster. But the Scots who were admitted to Ulster after 1603, whatever their ethnic origins, were easily distinguishable from Gaels, Scottish or Irish, by the fact that they spoke a dialect of English and were protestant in religion. Most of them came from the counties of Renfrew, Ayr, Wigtown and Kirkcudbright, where life was generally harder and rougher than in England, and were better prepared than the English for the rigours of pioneering in such a wild country as Ulster then was. Many English colonists expected too much of Ulster, and quite a number were so disappointed that they sold out and returned home. The Scots had the great advantage over the English that in south-west Scotland they had a source of reinforcements within easy reach; and during the critical seventeenth century they were repeatedly reinforced by fresh migrations from Scotland. The Scots had the right qualities for mastering their new environment—doggedness, self-reliance, realism, capacity for hard work, imperviousness to hostile opinion, unflagging determination to defend what they had gained, and the peculiar cohesion and discipline that they owed to their presbyterianism. The only church established by law in Ireland was the protestant episcopal, or anglican, church, the Irish equivalent of the Church of England, but in seventeenth-century Ulster there grew up alongside that church, in defiance of the law, a dissenting protestant system, presbyterianism, imported into Ulster by the Scots. Its ministers were severely dealt with by the government of Ireland after Wentworth became viceroy in 1633. In 1638, when Charles I's attempt from London to force an anglican liturgy on his presbyterian kingdom of Scotland was confronted by organised national resistance, there were sympathetic vibrations among the Ulster Scots, which were thought by Wentworth to pose a serious threat to English authority; and he expressed (5 January 1639) determination either to make them conform or to drive them out of Ulster back to Scotland. He overestimated the danger but illuminated the paradoxical position of the Ulster Scots. Their presbyterianism, unlike the anglicanism of the English colonists, stood at the opposite extreme to the catholicism of the Irish: its organisation was in principle republican, its theology was Calvinist, and its social code was puritan. Other groups of protestant dissenters emerged in the later-seventeenth and eighteenth centuries—quakers, independents, baptists, moravians, methodists—but numerically they were dwarfed by presbyterians, who by the eighteenth century outnumbered anglicans in Ulster. While a certain dourness was characteristic of Ulster protestantism generally, so also was a strong emotional tendency that sometimes found an outlet in mass hysteria, as in the evangelical revivals of the 1630s, of 1859, and of the early 1920s. Socially, while conformity to the established church was the hallmark of the landowning aristocracy, the presbyterian body consisted, in the main, of small freeholders, of tenant farmers, large and small, and of merchants and manufacturers. It remains true that the Ulster colony was the combined product of Scottish and English energy, enterprise and grit; that the valour of the defenders of Derry in the famous siege of 1689 is indivisible. But it was undoubtedly the Scottish rather than the English element that gave the colony its distinctive character and its distinctive place in history.

From the beginnings of the colony, religious categories were absolutely basic and inescapable, and this continues to be true. Religion in Ulster was, and is, important for its own sake, and differences between the rival theological systems of Rome, Geneva and Canterbury have always been an absorbing subject of controversy. But religious differentiation was also inseparable from, and religious denomination was the hallmark of, differing cultures and communities. Catholics belonged to the community that was of Gaelic stock, that had suffered defeat and (unjustly they believed) dispossession, that had been

8

forced into a mould of political impotence and of social and economic inferiority, that looked for deliverance to the overthrow of English power in Ireland, that longed for revenge on its supplanters and cherished an inheritance of bitter folk-memories. Conversely, protestants—anglicans, presbyterians and other protestant dissenters —belonged to the community that was colonial in origin, was economically and politically dominant, and that saw itself as the loyal British population, defending its superior culture against rebellious, priest-ridden, and barbarous natives, repeatedly frustrating, by unceasing vigilance and heroic struggle, attempts to despoil it and to destroy its British inheritance of civil and religious liberty, and justifying its right to ascendancy by the progressive agriculture, the thriving industry and the high standards of rural and urban living that distinguished Ulster from all the rest of Ireland. Of course the two communities and cultures did not remain absolutely separate, but the overmastering fact is that, to this day, neither has assimilated the other and that the dividing lines remain clear and distinct, not only in the heart but even on the ground: those areas of rural Ulster in which the seventeenth-century colony succeeded most are still the areas where protestants predominate, and catholics are the predominant element where it succeeded least. The denominational correlation can be carried even further: areas of presbyterian concentration generally signify areas of Scottish colonisation, while areas where anglicans preponderate are generally those where English colonists settled in strength. The six counties of the present Northern Ireland together represent the maximum area in terms of counties in which the colony became strongly entrenched, but even here there is a marked contrast between the two counties east of the Bann. Antrim and Down, where protestant settlers took root in overwhelming numbers, and the four west of the Bann, where they were more thinly spread. Antrim and Down today, taken together, have a large protestant majority, while the other four counties together have a small catholic majority, with protestants slightly preponderating in Londonderry and Armagh, and catholics in Tyrone and Fermanagh.

## III

## ULSTER AND THE UNITED IRISHMEN

In the eighteenth century, the classic age of catholic prostration and of protestant ascendancy, Ulster protestants lost much of their fear of catholics, and Ulster presbyterians began to resent the price they were made to pay for the ascendancy system. For the landowning and anglican minority treated presbyterians and other protestant dissenters—to whom they largely owed their survival—as only second-class citizens, excluding them from all civil and military offices under the crown, from local government, and in effect from parliament, and merely tolerating presbyterian worship. When to such grounds of embitterment were added the commercial depressions and agrarian grievances characteristic of the ascendancy age, presbyterians in disgust and indignation began to emigrate to the British colonies in America. The migration became a continuous flow which, by 1775, had drained off many thousands of the most vigorous presbyterians from Ulster. The presbyterian body was thus appreciably weakened and a strong radical element imported into America that played a notable part in winning American independence from Great Britain. The connections formed with America helped to stimulate in Ulster the growth of liberal and democratic ideas. In the last quarter of the eighteenth century Ulster was the fountain head of a liberal movement of protestant nationalism that aimed (a) at winning independence for the Irish parliament and making it a genuine representative assembly instead of the preserve of a corrupt ascendancy that it was, and (b) at removing civil and religious disabilities both from protestant dissenters and from catholics. This movement, largely middle-class but supported by a liberal element among the nobility and gentry, spread throughout Ireland, and found an effective political instrument in the Volunteers, a citizen army raised for home defence on local initiative to meet the danger of foreign invasion during the war of American independence. The Volunteers were highly successful in bringing pressure to bear on Britain, but the legal independence conceded by Britain to the Irish parliament was largely nullified by the fact that parliament remained unreformed, and the progress towards equality of citizenship stopped far short of emancipation for catholics. Both these deficiencies, in the era of the French revolution, became intolerable to Irish radicals, especially in Ulster, and this led to the first formulation of a democratic solution for the Irish problem.

The Society of United Irishmen was founded at Belfast in October 1791, by middle-class radicals, largely presbyterian, under the inspiration of a young Dublin protestant, Theobald Wolfe Tone. Tone's prescription for an independent, self-respecting and prosperous Ireland was 'to unite the whole people of Ireland, to abolish the memory of all past dissensions, and to substitute the common name of Irishman in place of the denominations of protestant, catholic and dissenter'.[1] Accepting this principle, the United Irishmen adopted a programme that in effect demanded national independence, the democratisation of parliament, and an end to all discrimination between citizens on the ground of religion. The movement won many adherents among middle-class protestants and catholics, and especially among Ulster presbyterians; and it contributed some of the leverage that brought about the catholic relief act of 1793, which conceded the parliamentary franchise to catholics on equal terms with protestants without allowing them to sit in parliament. This, however, marked the limit of United Irish success. Losing hope of achieving their aims by constitutional means, the more daring and resolute among them began in 1794 to prepare for rebellion with help from revolutionary France, with which Britain was now at war. Instead of 'a people united in the fellowship of freedom', the United Irishmen precipitated a new upsurge of sectarian hatred and violence.

What became a counter-revolutionary movement of protestants against the United Irish movement took shape in the Orange Society (later known as the Orange Order), which emerged out of the grassroots of communal con-

---

[1]*Life of Theobald Wolfe Tone . . . written by himself,* ed. W.T. Wolfe Tone (Washington, 1826), i, 51-2.

flict in Ulster. From the early 1760s peasant grievances were finding expression in intermittent violence organised by secret societies in various parts of Ireland against offending landlords and magistrates. The most notorious example of this rural terrorism was the Whiteboy movement in Munster. In Ulster, where the tenant-farmer class included both protestants and catholics, often bitter competitors for land, such violence merged into fighting between rival sectarian combinations. After an affray (the 'battle of the Diamond') near Loughgall, County Armagh, on 21 September 1795, between members of two such combinations, catholic Defenders and protestant Peep O'Day Boys, involving some hundreds of armed men, a new society was founded by the victorious protestants. Unlike the peasant organisations from which it sprang, this Orange Society combined protestant tenants with landowners in a secret organisation for the defence of protestant ascendancy, the constitution, and the social order, against both the Defenders, who were the most militant and widespread combinaton among the catholic peasantry, and the United Irishmen. As the United Irishmen became openly implicated in treason, upper-class protestants who had at first looked askance at Orangeism were drawn into it in large numbers, at the same time that the United Irish body was flooded with Defenders, attracted by its anti-ascendancy propaganda rather than by its appeal for unity between protestants and catholics. When the United Irishmen made their desperate attempt in 1798, the rising, except in Antrim and Down, had more of the character of a *jacquerie* than of a war of liberation, and with its suppression not only was the United Irish movement annihilated but it was fatally discredited in the eyes of protestants generally, and especially among Ulster liberals.

The sequel to the rising was the enforced union of Ireland with Great Britain. The union meant the termination of Ireland's existence as a separate state and the extinction of her parliament, which, however subservient, was the symbol of her separate identity. Partly by bribery, partly by threats, and partly by the compelling argument that the interests of the landowning class would best be served by a union, the Irish parliament was reluctantly induced to vote its own abolition. By the act of union of 1800 Ireland was merged juridically in the United Kingdom and given representation in the parliament of that kingdom. Outside parliament itself there was no strong or concerted

12

opposition to the union. The catholic bishops and the catholic upper and middle classes supported it, believing —erroneously as it proved—that it would quickly be followed by catholic emancipation. Ulster liberals were as disillusioned with the Irish parliament as with nationalist politics. On the other hand, Orange lodges in Ulster were among the most vociferous demonstrators against the union.

## IV

## ULSTER IN THE UNITED KINGDOM OF GREAT BRITAIN AND IRELAND, 1801-1921

The first half of the nineteenth century saw the reanimation of catholic Ireland and the rise of a new movement for national independence. The colonial nationalism of the eighteenth century, which had been led by liberal protestants from Grattan to Tone, was now replaced by a nationalism largely evoked and shaped by the towering personality of Daniel O'Connell, the greatest popular leader catholic Ireland had ever produced. O'Connell himself was a liberal, and his nationalism was non-sectarian, but it drew its support almost entirely from catholics, was closely identified with the catholic clergy, and won its crowning success in a mass movement for that emancipation which, despite the hopes held out to catholics on the eve of the union, was denied to them till 1829. As the catholic church emerged from the shadows of the penal laws to become the strongest social institution in Ireland, Ulster presbyterians and episcopalians, haunted by the nightmare of a catholic ascendancy replacing protestant ascendancy, composed their differences and joined forces in fervent and steady support of the union, and in implacable hostility to nationalism. The tradition of the United Irishmen, though never wholly extinguished, was eventually eclipsed by the Orange tradition—a tradition, in an age of rising democracy, of maintaining protestant ascendancy in an island where the overwhelming majority of the population was catholic but where protestants were strongly entrenched in one province, forming numerically rather more than half the population and in economic power being immeasurably superior to the other half. Ulster liberalism remained, pugnaciously critical of the Orangeist mentality but no longer identified with nationalism.

Economic developments in Ulster seemed to clinch the

unionist argument. The linen industry had experienced a unique development in Ulster ever since 1700, when the arrival of skilled textile workers, refugees from Picardy, had given it a new stimulus and set new standards. The industry both supplemented the economy of the small farmer and facilitated the growth of capital, which, towards the end of the eighteenth century was applied to the manufacture of cotton in and around Belfast by the new power-driven machinery. The industrial revolution thus introduced with cotton was soon transferred to linen, which adopted power spinning about 1830 and power weaving from 1850. Shipbuilding at Belfast began its prodigious modern career at Queen's Island in 1853; thereafter the industrial growth of the town was many-sided and spectacular. The increase in its population, from under 37,000 in 1821 to 100,000 in 1851, to 208,000 in 1881 and to 349,000 in 1901, is an index of this expansion. In marked contrast, Dublin in the nineteenth century reached its peak in 1851 with 258,000 and thereafter declined to 246,000 in 1891.

Industrialisation, initiated and sustained by protestants, the only source of substantial capital in Ulster, had the effect of accentuating Ulster's distinctiveness from the rest of Ireland and her community of interests with Britain. The industrialisation of the Lagan valley had no parallel in Ireland; and though it brought to Ulster a full share of the social suffering and the squalor inseparable from factory conditions in the nineteenth century, these were on balance outweighed by the advantages of a mixed agricultural and industrial economy, which enabled the rural population of the Lagan valley to survive the great famine with relatively little loss, in an age when the rural population of Ireland was generally declining. Belfast became an outpost of industrial Britain and the economic focus of Ulster. Her connections with the Clyde and the Mersey, on the one hand, and with the Ulster hinterland, on the other, became far more important than with Dublin. In the great age of railway building (1837-57) Belfast capitalists were far more interested in linking Belfast with Portadown, Enniskillen and Derry than in building a railway link with Dublin. If these captains of industry, all protestants, had needed any argument to turn them against nationalism, the economic argument would have been conclusive.

It was due basically to industrial development in Ulster that the great famine (1845-50) had less catastrophic effects there than in the rest of Ireland. The famine was less devastating because a smaller proportion of the rural population of Ulster belonged to the class that was wholly dependent on the potato. Ulster shared in the general decline of population from the famine onwards, but whereas, in the century after 1845, its population fell by one third, that of the other three provinces fell by one half. Ulster's contribution to the mass exodus, which accompanied and followed the famine and created a new Ireland in Britain and America, was much less than that of the rest of Ireland because Belfast and other towns were able to absorb a large part of the drift of population from the impoverished regions west of the Bann. Between 1841 and 1951 the population of this west-Ulster fell by 57%, whereas that of Antrim and Down rose by 27%. The eastward shift of population made little change in the percentage distribution of religious denominations west and east of the Bann, while strengthening the tendency of protestants to become concentrated in the Belfast area.

The British regime in Ireland under the union was marked by far-reaching, though sometimes long-delayed, reforms, in whose advantages Ulster shared with the rest of Ireland but in fuller measure:—reformed and progressive central administration, an efficient, highly professional, and generally impartial, police force (the Royal Irish Constabulary); successive enlargements of the parliamentary electorate; the reform of municipal corporations and of county government; a public system of elementary education, a new and non-sectarian system of university education, based on the Queen's Colleges of Belfast, Cork and Galway, and the subsidising and supervision of secondary education; the separation of church and state through the disestablishment and disendowment of the protestant episcopal church, reconstituted as a self-governing corporation, and the placing of all churches on a footing of complete legal equality; a special administration, the congested districts board, to care for the sub-marginal regions of the west; most epoch-making of all, radical changes in the land system which, beginning with the Gladstone reforms of 1870 and 1881 in landlord-tenant relations, eventually resulted in the conversion of the tenant farmers into peasant proprietors through the operation of state-aided land-purchase from 1885 onwards. This, the greatest social revolution of modern Ireland, was the response of the British parliament to a nationalist agitation directed against the landlord class not only as oppressors of the peasantry but also as the 'English garrison'. The protestant farmers of Ulster generally held aloof from the agitation, but they were just as ready as the catholics to take advantage of its results, even though their own relations with their landlords were exceptionally favourable.

The rise of peasant proprietorship destroyed the social influence of the old landed classes in three provinces without providing any alternative social leadership in the countryside; but in Ulster, where for a large part of the rural population a common protestantism tended to draw landlords and tenants together, the country gentry continued to exercise something of their former social influence after their former power as landlords had gone. Similarly the democratisation of county government in 1898, which replaced the old, oligarchic, grand-jury system by a system of elective councils (county, urban-district, and rural-district councils), transferred control of county affairs from protestant to catholic hands throughout most of Ireland but in Ulster left protestant control unimpaired over a wide area.

The system of primary education instituted by the state in 1831 was based on the principle of combined secular, and separate religious, instruction of the pupils, and was designed to educate protestant and catholic children in the same schools. The non-denominational theory underlying it was not acceptable to any of the principal churches in Ireland, but the educational advantages it offered to the children of the great mass of Irish people caused the catholic bishops to give the 'national' schools a cautious trial. The presbyterian and the anglican churches, on the other hand, were openly hostile, and the system only succeeded in Ulster after it had been remoulded on denominational lines, from 1840, in response to presbyterian pressure. The external forms of non-denominational education were preserved, but nearly all 'national' schools were in fact under denominational control. At the secondary-school level no attempt was made by the state to apply the 'national' system; and schools not under denominational control, such as the Royal Belfast Academical Institution (a typical product of Belfast liberalism), were a rarity. But on the level of higher education, while the catholic bishops demanded separate institutions under their own control, both the presbyterian and the anglican clergy came to accept the non-denominational principle as

17

exemplified in the Queen's Colleges founded at Belfast, Cork and Galway in 1845, and in Trinity College, Dublin, after the removal of all remaining religious disqualifications (except in the divinity school) in 1873.

It is often claimed that communal division in Northern Ireland has its roots in educational segregation. There is certainly some truth in this: if the 'national' schools had been genuinely non-denominational they would no doubt have helped to bridge the separation between protestants and catholics, whereas they probably helped to perpetuate communal division. But the fact was that deeply divided communities imposed their divisions on primary education, as on other social institutions, rather than that separate schools created a divided society. In Britain, where denominational education was the norm, society as a whole was not polarised between protestants and catholics. And whereas it is commonly supposed that the catholic church was principally responsible for educational segregation in Ireland, the truth is that the protestant churches, and especally the presbyterian church, had a larger share in defeating the attempt of the state to have children of Irish protestants and catholics educated together.

On the issue of higher education the presbyterian church itself was divided. A strong majority in the general assembly, the highest representative and governing body of that church, approved of Queen's College, Belfast, while a minority, inflexibly opposed to candidates for the presbyterian ministery receiving their general education in a non-denominational college, established Magee College at Derry on the opposite principle, but with the acquiescence of the majority. Queen's College, Belfast, won the confidence not only of the presbyterian church but also of the Church of Ireland for its scrupulous respect for denominational differences; and it achieved a success denied to its sister colleges at Cork and Galway, all three colleges being banned as 'godless' by the catholic church. After 1908 when the Belfast college acquired independent status as the Queen's University of Belfast, its importance as a meeting-place for all denominations was immensely enhanced through an informal concordat (the institution of a department of scholastic philosophy) with the catholic church, in consequence of which catholic students attended it in large and increasing numbers. This far-reaching change was made possible by the fact that the emergence of Queen's as a university was part of a general settlement of the university question under which catholic claims in the other three provinces were substantially satisfied.

Both protestants and catholics in Ulster thus shared in the benefits brought about both by state action in Ireland and by the industrial development of the north-east. But this did not win over catholics to unionism in significant numbers. While Ulster protestants, both liberals and conservatives, came to regard the idea of national independence with fear and loathing, Ulster catholics, especially from the time of the great famine, made it the essence of their political creed. In its classical formulation by Thomas Davis (a protestant), Gavan Duffy (a catholic), and others in the 1840s, Irish nationalism was a liberal, tolerant, magnanimous doctrine, that sought, in the spirit of the United Irishmen at their best, to build a new-style Irish nation, sober, self-reliant and self-governing, comprehending all creeds, classes and political and cultural traditions, transcending all past divisions, and respecting all the varied elements of the Irish inheritance. That was (and is) the theory of Irish nationalism, but the crucial fact was that, of the two great tasks the national movement set itself—to reconcile catholics and protestants, and to win Irish independence from Great Britain—far more progress was made towards the second than towards the first. Few protestants (there were always some) were converted to nationalism and nearly all nationalists were catholics. This situation was seen in its sharpest definition in Ulster: not only were Ulster protestants obsessively anti-nationalist but the nationalism of Ulster catholics tended to be of the kind that Gavan Duffy admitted he had cherished as a youth in Monaghan, when he had 'burned with desire to set up again the Celtic race and the catholic church'.[1] Orangeism in Ulster was thus matched by a no less intransigent catholic nationalism, which looked back in anger to a Gaelic Ulster long since overthrown.

The influx from rural Ulster into Belfast after the famine rapidly augmented catholic numbers in this citadel of protestantism so that by 1881 more than 30% of its population was catholic. But these catholics were generally the lowest strata of the working population, they were mostly segregated in certain parts of the city (notably the Falls area), and they tended to be pitted against protestant workers in fierce competition for jobs. The sectarian con-

[1] *Young Ireland* (London, 1880), p. 528.

flict that had precipitated the Orange movement in rural Armagh in 1795 was reproduced in a concentrated form in a mushrooming industrial city. Belfast, once so proud of its liberal reputation as the 'Athens of the north', earned a sombre notoriety from the 1830s as the scene of intermittent sectarian violence, in which protestant working-men fought savagely with catholic working-men while Irish police and British troops struggled in vain to keep the peace. To a much lesser degree Derry paralleled for north-west Ulster the role of Belfast in the Lagan valley: the rise of a shirt-making industry helped to provide employment for a depressed region, and the city expanded from 9,000 in 1821 to 19,000 in 1851, to 29,000 in 1881, and to 40,000 in 1901. But the paradox of Derry was that, as the scene of the most famous siege in the history of the British Isles (1689), it was one of the holiest places in Ulster protestant tradition, yet its population in the nineteenth century became increasingly catholic, till in 1881 catholics constituted more than half the total. The anniversary of the siege was usually a time of dangerous tension, which sometimes exploded into violence.

In the Ulster countryside, on the other hand, community conflict between catholics and protestants became less intense with the decline in population and the increasing security the small farmers acquired in their holdings through the land legislation from 1881 onwards. The conditions in which Orangeism and its catholic counterparts had arisen were thus gradually transformed, and the annual parades and ritual demonstrations with which Orangemen and catholics celebrated their rival anniversaries came to be a mutually acceptable part of the folk-life of rural Ulster rather than the mutual provocations to violence they tended to be in Belfast and other towns. Herein lies another paradox: the agrarian revolution that was turning Ulster farmers, protestant and catholic, into peasant proprietors, was itself both an expression of, and a stimulus to, that very nationalism to which Ulster protestants were so fervently opposed. Agrarian revolution, which in the rest of Ireland undermined protestant ascendancy, served in Ulster to strengthen the union with Britain by removing the only grounds of estrangement between protestant farmers and the landed aristocracy.

Nationalism pursued its objectives by two different methods and according to two different traditions, the one constitutional, the other revolutionary. Broadly they had the same aim. But constitutional nationalists, exploiting Irish representation in the British parliament, were prepared to accept a measure of domestic self-government as a basis of settlement, whereas revolutionary nationalists, organised after 1858 in a secret society, the Fenian, or Irish Republican, Brotherhood (I.R.B.), were separatists, who regarded Irish participation in the British parliament as futile and demoralising and dedicated themselves to overthrowing British authority by physical force as soon as circumstances should be favourable. And whereas constitutional nationalists tended to justify the claim to self-government on the ground that it was indispensable to good government, Fenians never wavered in their demand for national independence as an end in itself. Unlike previous revolutionary movements Fenianism drew its support not only from within Ireland but also from the catholic Irish whom emigration had transplanted abroad, especially in Britain and America. It was among Irish refugees in New York that Fenianism had its origins, and from then onwards Irish revolutionary movements have all had auxiliaries among Irish-Americans. Fenianism seemed to have shot its bolt with the abortive rising of 1867, but in fact it remained a pervasive and inextinguishable force below the surface of Irish politics—to its devotees, largely drawn from the working-classes, a flaming torch, summoning Irishmen to sacrifice everything in the holiest of causes; to unionists a shameful disease that had infected the catholic rabble with a lust for outrage and terrorism. The mass of catholics, including the catholic clergy, stood between these extremes, repelled by the Fenians' commitment to violence (though compared with to-day's men of violence they were generally humane and merciful), their defiance of the church, and their contempt for majority opinion, but admiring them for their courage, their self-sacrifice, and their constancy. It was in this context that a new essay in constitutional nationalism, the home-rule movement, was inaugurated in 1870 by Isaac Butt, a conservative protestant and former Orangeman, of Ulster origin. This movement, as led by an uncomparable political genius, Charles Stewart Parnell (also a protestant), came to have decisive though indefinable and ambiguous connections with the Fenian rank-and-file, most notably in the great land-agitation of 1879-82. In a sense the revolutionary movement was captured by the constitutional movement working through a militant and independent Irish party in parliament; and

21

for a generation it seemed that the future lay with the home-rulers. The support that Fenianism had hitherto received from the Irish in Britain and America was largely transferred to Parnell and his party. The progress of parliamentary democracy in the United Kingdom favoured the home-rulers, as the weight of catholic numbers in Ireland began to be reflected in Irish parliamentary representation. Before 1880 the majority of Irish M.P.s were protestant and before 1885 landowning. But in the general election of 1885, the first to be fought on a really popular franchise, this situation was transformed. Home-rulers won 85 of the 103 Irish seats at Westminister (a pattern that was to continue right down to 1918), and they fairly represented the solid mass of catholic opinion, lay and clerical, which was basically moderate and distinctively lower-middle class. It was this result that persuaded Gladstone, at the head of a large liberal majority in Great Britain, to commit his party to the home-rule cause and to make his epic attempt in 1886 to place home-rule on the statute book.

At this point, 1886, Ulster once again moved into the forefront of Irish and British politics. In the general election of 1885 home-rulers won 17 and unionists 16 of the 33 Ulster seats. The principal losers were the liberals, who had previously held 9 seats out of 29. Their annihilation was symbolic of the complete polarisation of Ulster politics, where liberalism had occupied a middle position between militant protestantism and militant catholicism. The Ulster liberal tradition did not entirely disappear, but it assumed a non-political character. The winners in the 1885 election, the home-rulers, carried all the seats in Donegal, Fermanagh, Monaghan and Cavan, and in each of the other counties except Antrim they carried one seat. The 'verdict of democracy', for the first time fully expressed in Ulster, pinpointed divisions that had their origins in the British colonisation of the seventeenth century, and set a pattern that continued till the end of the union and in a sense still remains. The petrifying intransigence of this situation caught the imagination of Winston Churchill in 1922:

Then came the Great War [of 1914-18]. Every institution, almost, in the world was strained. Great empires have been overturned. The whole map of Europe has been changed . . . The modes of thought of men, the whole outlook on affairs, the grouping of parties, all have encountered violent and tremendous changes in the deluge of the world. But as the deluge subsides and the waters fall short we see the dreary steeples of Fermanagh and Tyrone emerging once again. The integrity of their quarrel is one of the few institutions that has been unaltered in the cataclysm which has swept the world.[2]

The response of Ulster protestants to the 'verdict of democracy' was to prepare, by propaganda and organisation (including a great revival of the Orange Order), to thwart it, if necessary by physical force. Part of the protestant majority in the United Kingdom, they were determined not to become a minority in a self-governing, catholic Ireland, and in this attitude they were generally supported by the British conservative party. They wanted to keep all Ireland within the United Kingdom, but the idea had already taken shape among some that it might be necessary to partition the island and establish a separate administration for the north-east. Their threats of violent resistance to a home-rule measure were not put to the test in 1886, when Gladstone's first home-rule bill was defeated in the house of commons, nor in 1893, when his second attempt passed the commons but was overwhelmingly defeated by the lords. By that time an unexpected turn of events had seriously weakened the home-rule cause: Parnell, disgraced by the O'Shea divorce and deposed by the great majority of the party he had largely created, was dead (1891), and the party itself was torn by a demoralising split. It was not till 1910, when the Irish party was reunited under John Redmond and the liberal party was back in power under H. H. Asquith, that home rule again became a burning issue.

In 1912, a new home-rule bill (the third in a fateful series) passed the houses of commons and seemed certain (the veto power of the house of lords having been removed by the parliament act of 1911) of becoming law in 1914. It was at this juncture that unionist defiance in Ulster, uninhibitedly encouraged by the British conservative party, defeated and thereby discredited constitutional nationalism, and gave revolutionary nationalism the opportunity it had long awaited. In 1913 the establishment by the unionists of an Ulster Volunteer Force and preparations for the setting up of a provisional government for Ulster under Sir Edward Carson were quickly emulated in the south by the founding of the Irish National Volunteers, later the Irish Republican Army (I.R.A.). Asquith, who had

[2]*Hansard 5 (commons)*, cl, 1270 (16 Feb. 1922).

inherited Gladstone's commitment to home rule, had no clear policy when confronted by this crisis of parliamentary authority. He would not abandon his home-rule bill, but neither would he coerce the Ulster rebels. In the end, the threatened rebellion in Ulster, together with the outbreak of war in Europe, nullified the only home-rule scheme to reach the statute book. For the home-rule act of 1914 was accompanied by two fatal provisoes: it should not come into operation (1) till the war was over and (2) till parliament had had an opportunity by amending legislation to make special provision for Ulster. There followed in logical succession the Easter rising of 1916 in Dublin, the routing of the home-rule party by Sinn Féin (the constitutional front for the I.R.A.) in the general election of 1918, the war of independence (1919-21), the partitioning of Ireland by the Government of Ireland Act 1920, the Anglo-Irish treaty of 1921 and the civil war of 1922-3. The settlement that emerged in 1920-21, after a bitter and bloody struggle, was not what either unionists or nationalists had sought. The six Ulster counties in which the British colony had been most successful and in which protestants were most numerous were separated from the rest of Ireland under a home-rule parliament and administration of its own, corresponding to what the 1914 act had contemplated for all Ireland. The rest of Ireland was given dominion status as the Irish Free State, and thus, at the cost of partition, acquired through rebellion an independence that far exceeded the limits of the home rule denied to Ireland as a whole.

## V

# HOME RULE IN NORTHERN IRELAND, 1921-68

From 1921 a distinction has to be made between the historic province of Ulster, comprising nine counties, and the six north-eastern counties that were combined to form the political unit of Northern Ireland. Geographically, and to some extent culturally, the nine counties of Ulster are still an identifiable region, but administratively the six counties of Northern Ireland have become increasingly distinct from the three bordering counties (Donegal, Monaghan and Cavan) which are included in the Republic. For most purposes the term Ulster has come to be used within the six counties as interchangeable with Northern Ireland.

Home rule in Northern Ireland did not solve the Ulster question, but it was far from being the total failure its detractors have alleged. Administration in the north, with the cooperation and financial backing of the British government, has in many ways been conducted on higher standards than in the south and has a better record of achievement, exemplified by education at all levels, the social services, the Northern Ireland Housing Trust, motorways, the Public Record Office, the Ulster Museum and Art Gallery, the Ulster Folk Museum, and the Ulster Orchestra. In primary education, whereas the Irish Free State took over the existing system while abandoning its non-denominational forms, Northern Ireland made a determined effort to create a real non-denominational system under the control of local education authorities, and achieved a large measure of success with the schools that had been under protestant management. The catholic schools all opted to remain outside the system of county control, and were therefore ineligible for building grants under the education act of 1923; but this restriction was successively relaxed, and in recent years the voluntary schools have received much the same financial support as those inside the state system. In such fields all classes and creeds have shared the benefits of improved administration in a Northern Ireland under home rule.

On the other hand the age-long division between protestants and catholics remained, though, especially from the sixties, much was done to build bridges between the two communities. With improving conditions and rising expectations, catholics resented more deeply than ever the fact that they were treated only as second-class citizens. Though till recently the official unionist attitude was to deny that discrimination was practised against catholics, and though charges of discrimination were often ill-founded, the reality of catholic grievances was established beyond all doubt by the efforts of Captain Terence O'Neill as prime minister (1963-9) to remedy them and by the sectarian conflict that this precipitated. It thus happened that the tentative findings on discrimination reached by two quakers, who in 1959-60, before Captain O'Neill became prime minister, investigated the problem of sectarian division in Northern Ireland[1], were fully corroborated by a commission appointed on his initiative in March 1969 to inquire into disturbances that had occurred in and since the preceding October. The commission was headed by a Scottish judge, Lord Cameron, and its two other members were Sir John Biggart, professor of pathology in Queen's University, Belfast, and Mr James Campbell, principal lecturer in education, St Joseph's Training College, Belfast. It was a well-balanced trio of very able and experienced men, and their report[2] is a landmark in the history of Northern Ireland.

The root causes of discrimination against catholics were protestant distrust and fear. Though protestants in Northern Ireland were in a majority of two-thirds, they were all too well aware of being in a minority in all-Ireland, and were all too ready to see the catholics in their midst as a kind of fifth column, forever bent on ending partition and merging the north in a reunited Ireland in which they would be part of an overwhelmingly catholic majority. The protestant fears thus perpetuated were reinforced by the fact, generally exaggerated, that catholics were becoming an increasing percentage of the

[1]D. P. Barritt and C. F. Carter, *The Northern Ireland problem: a study in group relations* (London, 1962).

[2]*Disturbances in Northern Ireland: report of the commission appointed by the governor of Northern Ireland* (Cmd 532; Belfast: H.M.S.O., 1969); hereafter cited as *Cameron report.*

population of Northern Ireland—they increased from 33.5% in 1926 to 34.9% in 1961. The hostile activities of the I.R.A. against Northern Ireland[3] repeatedly showed that protestant fears were justified. The lesson that traditional unionists drew from all this was that protestant supremacy must be maintained at all costs: 'not an inch' must be yielded to the enemy within the gate.

The inferior civil status of catholics was exemplified in two ways.

(1) Democracy in Northern Ireland was regarded by the majority as realised in 'a protestant parliament for a protestant people'—a phrase coined by Sir James Craig, later Lord Craigavon, who was Northern Ireland's first prime minister. Instead of a real party system, based on differences of social policy and principles and assuming alternations of the party or parties in power, parliamentary life in Northern Ireland was sterilised into the perpetual rule of one party. This 'Ulster Unionist Party', closely connected with the Orange Order, included all varieties of 'loyalists', claimed to cater for the whole spectrum of social interests, and justified its monopoly of power by the continuing need to defend the state against the danger of subversion by the 'disloyal' minority, with which the parliamentary opposition was associated. For this frozen situation catholics were themselves partly responsible because they could never agree frankly to accept the constitution of Northern Ireland and to cooperate with the majority in making the best of it. Catholic alienation from the Stormont parliament (the parliament of Northern Ireland, located at Stormont, on the eastern outskirts of Belfast) was increased when, in 1929, proportional representation, which had hitherto been used in Northern Ireland elections, was abolished in favour of single-member constituencies. The change was probably due to unionist fears that P.R. would give rise to protestant splinter-groups, but to the catholics it was seen as a move to deprive them of a potential advantage. A symbol of continuing protestant supremacy and an object of particular resentment to catholics was the Ulster Special Constabulary (the 'B Specials'), a part-time paramilitary force created for the purpose of countering I.R.A. terrorism, recruited exclusively from protestants, and identified with sectarian harassment of catholics. The 'B Specials' were distinct from the regular police, the Royal

---

[3]See below, p. 46.

Ulster Constabulary (R.U.C.), which, though armed, was a civilian force, and, though largely composed of protestants, included a substantial percentage of catholics.

The executive in Northern Ireland was from the beginning invested by parliament with a formidable armoury of special powers to deal with subversive activities. The Civil Authorities (Special Powers) Act (N.I.) 1922 gave the minister of home affairs power (which he might delegate to his parliamentary secretary or to any police officer) 'to take all such steps . . . as may be necessary for preserving the peace and maintaining order'. The obligation was placed on any person knowing, or having good grounds for believing, that some other person was contravening the act to inform the minister accordingly. The burden of proving that anything alleged to be in contravention of the act was in fact done by lawful authority was to rest on the accused. All powers conferred by the act on the R.U.C. were also made exercisable by the Ulster Special Constabulary. Regulations appended in a schedule to the act, supplemented or altered by other regulations made subsequently by the minister of home affairs, provided for the detailed application of the act to persons suspected of behaving, or to things suspected of being used, 'in any way prejudicial to the preservation of the peace or maintenance of public order'. Thus discretionary power was given to the police to enter and search any suspected house, to stop any suspected vehicle on the road, to search any person suspected of carrying arms, to suppress publications prejudicial to the maintenance of order, and to arrest any person without warrant and detain him for forty-eight hours for interrogation. Any person authorised by the civil authority or by any police constable or by any member of the armed forces might arrest any suspect without warrant, and anyone so arrested might be detained in prison or elsewhere until discharged by direction of the attorney general or brought before a court of summary jurisdiction. A suspected person might, at the discretion of the minister of home affairs, be subjected to restrictions as to residence, movement and otherwise, or be interned in prison or elsewhere, provided that any representations from an internee must be duly considered by an advisory committee appointed by the minister. It was made an offence under the act to be a member of the I.R.B., the I.R.A., the U.V.F.,[4] and other unlawful associations.

[4]See below, pp. 72-3.

The act, made at a time of great emergency, when the new government was struggling to establish its authority against republican attacks, was, and has continued to be, specially directed against the I.R.A. It was renewed annually till 1928, when it was extended for five years, at the end of which, in 1933, it was made permanent. It has very seldom been used against protestants, for the obvious reason that, until recently, protestants were not involved in subversive activities against the government. But to catholics the act was a festering grievance, because it was they who suffered whenever the police, in pursuit of the I.R.A. or of information about the I.R.A., exercised their powers of forcible entry, search or interrogation, or whenever suspects were interned. The act was severely criticised by liberal and legal opinion in Britain; and in 1936 a private commission of inquiry set up by the [British] National Council for Civil Liberties issued a report that strongly condemned both the principle and the administration of the act. No circumstances could justify the embodiment of such drastic powers into the permanent law of the land. The perpetuation of these powers amounted to a surrender by parliament of its law-making functions to the executive and the abrogation of the rule of law by 'the substitution of the arbitrary power of the executive for the legally defined and protected rights of the subject'. The commission found that the government of Northern Ireland had used the act so as to secure the 'domination' of the unionists and to restrict the lawful activities of their opponents, with the result that legitimate movements were driven underground and moderate opponents of government were turned into extremists.[5]

The commission's report was not a judicial or an authoritative document, and it produced a storm of controversy. But the commissioners were persons of some eminence and standing (they included Margery Fry, a former principal of Somerville College, Oxford, and two former liberal M.P.s, Major William McKeag, solicitor, and E. L. Mallalieu, barrister), and their findings showed a concern in Britain about the special powers act which was to continue unabated to the present time. The repeal of the act was a major item in the programme of reforms

[5]*Report of a commission of inquiry appointed to examine the purpose and effect of the Civil Authorities (Special Powers) Acts (Northern Ireland) 1922 & 1923* (London: National Council for Civil Liberties, 1936).

which, thirty years afterwards, the present Northern Ireland Civil Rights Association was formed to promote. The Cameron commission in 1969 examined the working of the act and pointed out that such practices as arrest without warrant and indefinite imprisonment without trial, the presumption that an accused person was guilty until he proved himself innocent, interference with the privacy of person and home, were contrary to the Universal Declaration of Human Rights; and described as a 'powerful contention' the view of the Society of Labour Lawyers that the permanent retention of an act that gave powers to the police so much at variance with the rights of the citizen was contrary to a fundamental principle of English law. On the other hand the danger that the act was designed to meet had not ceased, for the I.R.A. had mounted a new campaign of violence as recently as 1956-62, 'and there is evidence that its activities still continue and its objectives remain the same, even if temporarily its tactics vary'. Moreover from 1966 the activities of a secret organisation of protestant extremists, the Ulster Volunteer Force (which was declared illegal under the act) had strengthened the case for special powers. Finally the Cameron commission suggested that these powers were very similar to those conferred by Dáil Eireann on the government of the Republic by the Offences Against the State Act 1939.[6] This was correct, and the special powers in question were, as in Northern Ireland, devised primarily to combat the I.R.A. But in the Republic the exercise of these special powers has not, as in Northern Ireland, been associated with sectarian conflict and the problem of a divided society.

(2) Catholics were persistently discriminated against in local government through the maintenance of a ratepayers' franchise instead of universal adult suffrage as in Great Britain, and through the jerrymandering of constituencies; in the allocation of houses by local authorities; and in access to local government posts as well as to jobs in private firms, the latter grievance aggravated by high levels of unemployment, especially in the areas west of the Bann where catholics preponderate. Here the position of Derry was critical. With a population of which catholics formed 67% and a county borough council in which 60% of the seats were held by protestants, it was the most blatant example of manipulating ward-boundaries

[6]*Cameron report*, pp 12-13, 62-3, 77-81, 104-7.

in the interests of unionist control. In 1968 only 30% of the administrative, clerical and technical employees of Derry Corporation were catholics, and of the ten best-paid posts only one was held by a catholic.[7] The economy of Derry, which had long been subject to sharp fluctuations, was adversely affected by partition, and its level of male unemployment was exceptionally high. The government's decision, following the Lockwood committee's report of 1965, to locate a second Ulster university at Coleraine rather than at Derry, where Magee University College had been in existence for a century, was a bitter disappointment to Derry people. They had hoped that a large and adequately financed modern university would bring a much-needed boost to Derry's economy and to its morale; and it is possible that if the New University of Ulster, instead of being as it is at Coleraine, an outlier of the British university system, had been located at Derry and adapted to the special needs of the north-west, it could have been a source of revival and reconciliation in a depressed and bitterly divided area.

In other local government areas—Armagh urban district, Omagh urban district and County Fermanagh—a catholic majority in the population was artificially turned into a large protestant majority in the elective council; and in Dungannon urban and rural districts, a very small protestant majority in the population held two-thirds of the seats on the council. Otherwise the membership of local councils tended to reflect the religious distribution of their localities, and electoral swings of the pendulum at local government level were as rare as in elections for the Stormont parliament. In general, unionist-controlled councils used their powers of appointment and of allocating houses to benefit protestants; and the converse was also true. Moreover houses were built and allocated by the local authorities in such a way as not to disturb the electoral balance; for example in Derry, the large new housing estate of the Creggan, in the west ward, was used almost exclusively to rehouse catholics. This policy helped to strengthen and perpetuate the segregation of protestants and catholics which other and centuries-old conditions had created. Finally the nature of the local government franchise tended to discriminate against the poorer sections of the population and especially, therefore, against catholics. For unlike the parliamentary franchise, it was

[7]Ibid., pp 13, 59-60, 64.

open only to occupiers of dwelling-houses, and thus excluded nearly a quarter of those entitled to vote at Stormont elections. The introduction of universal suffrage would have altered political control in few local councils, but the sense of rankling injustice felt by catholics over this issue was not the less strong, and found expression in the emotive and infectious slogan 'one man one vote', which the Northern Ireland Civil Rights Association adopted as one of its battle-cries in 1968.

The 'not an inch' mentality remained a characteristic of government in Northern Ireland under its first three prime ministers—Lord Craigavon (1921-40), J.M. Andrews (1940-43), and Lord Brookeborough (1943-63). But the fourth prime minister, Captain Terence O'Neill (1963-9), realised that radical changes in unionist thinking and unionist policy were urgently necessary if the unresolved conflict in Northern Ireland was not to explode, and if the unionist regime was not to forfeit the goodwill —and the financial support—of Great Britain. Tracing his aristocratic ancestry from both planter and Gaelic stock, bearing the most famous of Gaelic-Ulster names but upper-class English in education and social pattern, forward-looking and flexibly minded, for seven years a progressive minister of finance, he saw it as his role to win over the minority to loyal acceptance of a Northern Ireland reformed and renovated on liberal lines. In a courageous effort to remedy catholic grievances he pioneered a policy of community reconciliation combined with an energetic programme of attracting new industries, and an imaginative gesture of friendliness to the Republic. But his innovations came too slowly and too late to conciliate the catholics, and too fast and too soon for the hard-line unionists who eventually made his position untenable. It was over the issue of discrimination in housing in Caledon, County Tyrone, that a gesture of protest (20 June 1968) by a nationalist M.P. at Stormont, Mr Austin Currie, sparked off a series of civil rights demonstrations, beginning with a march from Coalisland to Dungannon on 24 August, which opened up the present era of violence in Northern Ireland.

## VI

## THE DISTURBANCES OF 1968-9 AND THE GOVERNMENT'S REFORM PROGRAMME

The civil rights marches, in conscious imitation of similar movements in America and elsewhere, were sponsored by the Northern Ireland Civil Rights Association. This was an open and non-violent pressure-group founded at Belfast in February 1967, whose members, largely catholic and representing a variety of political interests, were united only in promoting a programme of specific reforms as follows: (a) a points system to ensure a fair allocation of local-authority housing; (b) legislation against discrimination in local-government employment, and machinery to deal with grievances arising out of local government; (c) the redrawing of electoral boundaries by an independent commission to ensure fair representation; (d) universal adult suffrage in local government elections; (e) repeal of the special powers act; (f) the withdrawal of the Public Order (Amendment) Bill then before parliament, which, among other provisions, proposed to extend the powers of the minister for home affairs over public processions; (g) the disbandment of the 'B specials'.[1] But the Civil Rights Association from an early stage was infiltrated by left-wing and republican elements, which, the Cameron commission found,

> were ready to use the civil rights movement to further their own purposes, and were ready to exploit grievances in order to provoke and foment, and did provoke and foment, disorder and violence in the guise of supporting a non-violent movement[2]

The violent reaction of the police to a civil rights march

[1]*Cameron report,* pp 18-19, 78.
[2]Ibid., p. 92.

in Derry on 5 October 1968 drew world attention to the Derry situation and at once resulted in the mobilising of moderate opinion among local catholics. The Derry Citizens' Action Committee (the first of many such groups in Northern Ireland), formed on 9 October with aims very similar to those of the Civil Rights Association, was the outcome of local initiative, and it quickly earned distinction for integrity in its endeavours to restrain mob-violence while making use of non-violent techniques of protest, including the 'sit-down', to advance its objects. Its chairman, Mr John Hume, a former schoolteacher and moving spirit in the Derry Credit Union and the Derry Housing Association, emerged as a dedicated and responsible popular leader, articulate, resolute and fearless. In the course of the next few months he became widely known on the television screen for the energy and the moral authority with which, in the thick of tumultuous crowds on the streets of Derry, he sought to curb the angry passions of his fellow-catholics. With him was closely associated Mr Ivan Cooper, a local protestant.

In the face of the civil rights crisis, and under pressure from Westminister, Captain O'Neill succeeded in persuading his cabinet to agree to a five-point programme of reform, which he announced on 22 November: (1) a fair allocation of local-authority housing was to be secured by a points system; (2) new methods were to be introduced to facilitate the investigation of citizens' grievances including the appointment of an 'ombudsman'; (3) the Derry county borough council and the Derry rural district council were to be superseded by a broadly-based development commission; (4) the company vote in local government elections was to be abolished, and a comprehensive reform and modernisation of local government, including electoral areas, was to be brought into effect by the end of 1971; (5) the special powers act was to be reviewed and clauses conflicting with the United Kingdom's international obligations were to be withdrawn as soon as possible. Captain O'Neill had tried in vain to win cabinet acceptance of universal adult suffrage ('one man one vote') in local government elections; he gained his point, however, in the following April, when 'one man one vote' was accepted for local elections. This and the reforms of the five-point programme were a real attempt to meet the demands of the civil rights movement, and they at once eased the tension in Derry, but their remedial value was largely nullified by renewed violence.

Civil rights demonstrations at Dungannon (23 November and 4 December) and at Armagh (30 November) encountered violent opposition from protestant militants which the police were unable to control. A march from Belfast to Derry (1-4 January 1969) promoted, against the advice of the civil rights leaders, by the People's Democracy, an amorphous left-wing movement based on students of Queen's University, Belfast, was harassed along its seventy-five mile route by protestant extremists. The marchers, numbering about 500, were ambushed and viciously attacked at Burntollet Bridge, near Claudy, County Londonderry, on 4 January, by an organised body of 200 protestants, armed with cudgels and iron bars and well supplied with missiles in the shape of stones, bricks and bottles. The wholly unarmed marchers suffered heavy casualties, some requiring hospital treatment. The attack was in part a reaction to rioting in Derry the night before, which was believed by protestants, erroneously, to have been the work of members and supporters of the People's Democracy. But what gave the Burntollet affair immediate notoriety was the fact that a high proportion of the attackers were 'B Specials' and that the police did little to protect the marchers. Some eighty R.U.C. men were present, but though they watched the ambushers gathering near the bridge they took no preventitive action against them; and though, once the attack began, they tried to protect the marchers at the front, the main body was left to the mercy of the attackers. The Cameron commission, which coolly and critically investigated the matter a few months later, concluded that the eighty police could not have stopped the violence and that they were as much taken by surprise as the marchers by the rapid build-up of the counter-demonstrators. But, with every reason to fear serious disorder, 'they neglected to make adequate use of their opportunities for forward planning to meet and deal with the events which occurred and might have been foreseen'. The violence at Burntollet was repeated when the march reached Derry, and the behaviour of the police was still more partizan. The Cameron commission reported:

We have to record with regret that our investigations have led us to the unhesitating conclusion that on the night of 4-5 January a number of policemen were guilty of misconduct which involved assault and battery, malicious damage to property in streets in the predominantly catholic Bogside area,

35

giving reasonable cause for apprehension of personal injury among other innocent inhabitants, and the use of provocative sectarian and political slogans.[3]

Burntollet and its sequel, following on similar behaviour by the police at Derry on 5 October and subsequently elsewhere, did irreparable damage to the reputation of the R.U.C. in the eyes of the catholics of Northern Ireland. The Cameron commission found that 'one very unfortunate consequence of these breaches of discipline . . . was to add weight to the feeling, which undoubtedly exists among a certain proportion of the catholic community, that the police are biased in their conduct against the catholic demonstrators in demonstrations'.

Thus it is said that when the police have to interpose themselves between unionist demonstrators on the one hand and a similar body of catholic or civil rights demonstrators on the other, they invariably face the latter and have their backs to the former. The corollary is that if stones or other missiles are thrown from the unionist crowd the police do not see who is responsible, while they concentrate their attention against the non-unionists. The fact is undoubted; the reason given for it— that unionists being loyalists do not attack the police—is not accepted as satisfactory or a sufficient reply to the charge of partizan bias. This complaint however is not confined to the events under investigation but is one of general application and long standing.[4]

One effect of the People's Democracy march to Derry, which was probably intended by its leaders, was to polarise extreme elements and weaken the position of moderate reformers. The hard-line unionist reaction against Captain O'Neill, which had caused him to dismiss Mr William Craig, his minister of home affairs, on 11 December, was carried a stage further on 23 January by the resignation of Mr Brian Faulkner, his minister of commerce, in protest against the cabinet's decision to set up a commission of inquiry (the Cameron commission) into the recent disturbances. When a number of back-bench unionists demanded Captain O'Neill's resignation, he at once called a general election for 24 February, and he made the election the occasion for committing the unionist party to the principle of equality of rights and duties for all citizens:

[3]*Cameron report*, p. 73.
[4]Ibid., p. 74.

The Ulster Unionist Party believes in an Ulster in which the obligations and rights of all citizens will be fully recognised. It expects of all citizens that loyalty towards the state which is due when the institutions of that state have the expressed support of a clear majority. It seeks from every individual a proper sense of responsibility and whole-hearted participation in the life of the state. . . . The party acknowledges and proclaims the right of all citizens to . . . full equality in the enjoyment of health, education, and other social benefits and to the protection of authority against every kind of injustice.[5]

But the result of the election was that, though unionists won 36 of the 52 seats, as in the preceding general election, they were split between 24 pro-O'Neill and 12 anti-O'Neill members. This, followed in April by further sectarian disturbances in Derry and by explosions at the Belfast city reservoir and at electricity installations (later proved to be the work of protestant extremists), ensured Captain O'Neill's resignation, which was formally accepted on 1 May. He had won the confidence and raised the hopes of catholics as no prime minister of Northern Ireland had ever done, and as neither of his successors had any possibility of doing. His immediate successor, his cousin, Major James Chichester-Clark, whose defection over the 'one man one vote' issue had been the final blow, had not been in office three months before Derry and Belfast were ravaged by communal violence which the police were unable to control and which forced him to call for the intervention of British troops.[6] At this point, August 1969, the northern scene became overshadowed by the danger of sectarian civil war.

The disturbances of October 1968-January 1969, then, arose out of the long-standing civil grievances of the catholic minority. Non-violent civil rights demonstrations were met by protestant violence, in the handling of which the police failed in their obligation of impartiality. The civil rights agitation provided the leverage that enabled

[5]Quoted in *A commentary on the programme of reforms for Northern Ireland* (New Ulster Movement publication 2, June 1971), p. [4].
[6]The violence of March-August 1969 was fully investigated by the Scarman tribunal (Sept. 1969-Feb. 1972); see bibliography, below, p. 121.

Captain O'Neill to push his reform programme through the unionist parliamentary party. He remained in office only long enough to see the setting up (5 February) of the Derry Development Commission which, composed of well-chosen catholics and protestants in a fair proportion, opened up new hopes for a depressed and distracted locality.[7] The rest of his projected reforms, apart from the question of the special powers act, were carried out or put in train by his successor before the end of 1969. A parliamentary commissioner for administration ('ombudsman'), to hear citizens' complaints against central government departments (24 June),[8] and a commissioner for complaints with a corresponding role in relation to local authorities (25 November) were established.[9] A model points-scheme for public-authority housing was introduced by the ministry of development.[10] The franchise for local electors was assimilated to the parliamentary franchise by a new electoral act.[11]

Other and related reforms were introduced by Major Chichester-Clark and by his successor Mr Faulkner. Following the entry of British troops into Derry and Belfast, the governments of Northern Ireland and the United Kingdom issued a joint statement (the 'Downing Street Declaration' of 20 August 1969), in which the British government welcomed the reforms already made 'as demonstrating the determination of the Northern Ireland government that there shall be full equality of treatment for all citizens', and both governments expressed agreement on the vital necessity of maintaining the momentum of reform. They also declared that 'every citizen in Northern Ireland is entitled to the same equality of treatment and freedom from discrimination as obtains in the rest of the United Kingdom, irrespective of political views or religion'. In communiqués of 29 August and 10 October the Northern Ireland government made specific commitments to reform over a large range of topics, and action was taken accordingly. A committee to advise on the police—the Hunt committee—was appointed

---

[7]*Statutory rules and orders of Northern Ireland, 1969*, pp 135-6; *Ulster year book, 1972*, pp 118-19.

[8]Parliamentary Commissioner Act (N.I.) 1969 (24 June).

[9]Commissioner for Complaints Act (N.I.) 1969 (25 Nov.).

[10]*A record of constructive change* (Cmd 558; Belfast: H.M.S.O., 1971).

[11]Electoral Law Act (N.I.) 1969 (25 Nov.).

on 26 August, and in accordance with its report (3 October) it was decided to establish a police authority representative of the whole community, to transform the R.U.C. into a 'civilianised' and unarmed police force, relieved of all military duties, to replace the 'B Specials' with a part-time, civilian, police reserve, and to establish a locally recruited and part-time security force under army control, the Ulster Defence Regiment, to assist the army in such duties as guarding key installations, carrying out patrols, and operating check points. The new police organisation was instituted by the Northern Ireland parliament in March, while the Ulster Defence Regiment, which became operational on 1 April, was set up by the British government.[12] In April 1971 it was decided to relieve the police of the duty of prosecuting in summary offences by instituting a system of independent public prosecutors.[13] A ministry of community relations was established in October 1969,[14] and a community relations commission, independent of the government in November.[15] It was decided in October to set up a central housing authority, and in view of this decision and of proposals for reshaping local government a review body was appointed on 7 December, under the chairmanship of Mr Patrick Macrory, which reported on 28 May 1970.[16] All public-authority house-building and house allocation were made the responsiblity of a new central organisation, the Northern Ireland Housing Executive, instituted in February 1971.[17] A radical re-shaping of the entire system of local government was announced in December 1970, in pursuance of the Macrory report. Certain major functions such as health and social services, education, planning, roads, water, electricity, fire services and electoral arrangements were to be administered for Northern Ireland as a single unit through five area boards, while functions of a more localised character were to be the responsibility of twenty-six new district councils. An independent boundary commissioner, Mr F. A. L. Harrison, Q.C., was appointed in March 1971 to recommend boundaries and names for the new districts and also for the electoral divisions or wards

[12]Police Act (N.I.) 1970 (26 Mar.).

[13]*A record of constructive change* (Cmd 558), p. 2.

[14]Ministry of Community Relations (N.I.) Act 1969 (28 Oct.).

[15]Community Relations Act (N.I.) 1969 (11 Nov.).

[16]*Review body on local government in Northern Ireland 1970 . . . report* (Cmd 546; Belfast: H.M.S.O., 1970).

[17]Housing Executive Act (N.I.) 1971 (25 Feb.).

into which they were to be divided.[18] The creation and introduction of this single-tier system of local government, designed to replace the complex system of seventy-three local authorities unchanged since 1898,[19] was a laborious and intricate task, requiring much new legislation, but it was substantially completed according to plan by May 1973, when elections were held under the new arrangements for the twenty-six new councils. Various schemes were adopted to ensure fair representation of minorities at the elective levels of government, and to prevent discrimination on religious or political grounds in all forms of public employment[20], and it was made a statutory offence to incite to religious hatred.[21]

Alongside these reforms on an administrative, social and political level the government was endeavouring to grapple with the economic problems of Northern Ireland, and especially to reduce unemployment. In May 1968, before the current disturbances began, it had commissioned three independent consultants, Sir Robert Matthew (professor of architecture, University of Edinburgh), J. R. Parkinson (professor of economics, University of Nottingham), and Thomas Wilson (professor of political economy, University of Glasgow), to draft a five-year programme of economic development beginning in 1970. Their recommendations, published in June 1970 as the Northern Ireland Development Programme, 1970-75, were accepted by the government, which took the necessary steps to put them into effect. The programme dealt with all aspects of its subject: 'employment, industrial development, industrial training, industrial relations, housing, physical development and location strategy, mobility, amenity, tourism, agriculture, transport and communications, education, health and welfare, and administration'. It prescribed a two-fold strategy of development for (a) the relatively prosperous industrial region of the Greater Belfast area (including Antrim, Carrickfergus, Craigavon, Bangor and Newtownards), and (b) the rest of Northern Ireland, a largely agricultural area where the problem was to create industrial jobs to absorb the unemployed. In this latter area Derry and Ballymena were designated centres for accelerated industrial growth, and elsewhere

[18]*A record of constructive change* (Cmd 558), pp 9-10; Local Government Boundaries Act (N.I.) 1971 (23 Mar.).
[19]See above, p. 17.
[20]*A record of constructive change,* pp 4-7.
[21]Incitement to Hatred Act (N.I.) 1970 (2 July).

development was to be concentrated in eight key-centres, four of them in the west (Strabane, Omagh, Dungannon and Enniskillen) and four in the east (Coleraine, Larne, Downpatrick and Newry). The whole programme was estimated to cost about £2,400,000,000 (at 1969 prices).

Finally a move was made by Mr Faulkner in June 1971 to modify the hitherto unbroken monopoly of political power by the unionist party. He announced in the house of commons a new committee-system through which opposition members would be able to share in the work of government. Alongside the public accounts committee, three new 'functional committees'—for social services, for environmental services, and for industrial services—would be set up, consisting of about nine members each, broadly representative of party strength in the house of commons. The chairmanship of each of the four committees would be a salaried post, committee members would be paid a fee for attendance, and at least two of the four chairmen would be drawn from the opposition. Mr Faulkner also took the positive step of appointing Mr David Bleakley, a Belfast schoolmaster and former labour M.P., as minister of community relations in March 1971. He was the first member of the Northern Ireland Labour Party to enter the cabinet, and he resigned after six months over the issue of internment. In October Mr Faulkner brought the first catholic into the cabinet—Dr Gerard B. Newe, who since 1948 had been secretary of the Northern Ireland Council of Social Service, and, like Mr Bleakley, was well known as a man dedicated to the cause of peace, welfare and reconciliation. His appointment as minister of state was terminated by the introduction of direct rule in March 1972, but not before he had shown great courage in face of bitter denounciation from nationalists who regarded his acceptance of office as the act of a quisling.

Why, in face of all this flood of reform, which in a few years has gone so far to meet civil rights demands and has done and is doing so much to modernise the institutions and expand the economic life of Northern Ireland, did disturbances not subside but became uncomparably worse in and after 1969? Partly the answer is that the unionist reforms of 1968 and after were too long overdue, so that they won no gratitude from the minority and did little to remove their sense of alienation. It was all too obvious that reforms were the response both to the pressure of events within Northern Ireland

and to pressure from the British government; they proved the reality of catholic grievances but had little immediate bearing on the lives of ordinary people. Partly the reforms failed in their immediate purpose because the minority continued to be excluded from political power and lacked confidence in Captain O'Neill's successors, however much they showed willingness to remedy catholic grievances. The catholics continued to see the police as their enemies even after the Hunt reforms had been put into effect, and government hopes that catholics would join the reorganised R.U.C. in increased numbers were disappointed. When Mr Faulkner did offer an instalment of power-sharing to the opposition, his intention was defeated by the withdrawal (15 July 1971) of opposition members from parliament in protest against government reaction to intensified violence. His appointment of Dr Newe brought him even less political advantage than that of Mr Bleakley. Underlying all these causes of the failure of reform to allay discontent was the unyielding resistance of right-wing unionists to what they regarded as a policy of appeasement. It was this, more than any other single cause, that frustrated Captain O'Neill's good intentions and proved no less injurious to his successors, who themselves had moved over from a right-wing position to the moderate and reforming unionism to which he had committed the party. But even if there had been solid unionist support for the policy of liberal reform, it is questionable whether the problem of Northern Ireland could have been solved in 1968-9 within a unionist context. This brings us to the nationalist factor in the situation and to the all-Ireland context of the problem.

## VII

## NORTHERN IRELAND AND THE IRISH REPUBLIC,
### 1921-69

Over and above their particular grievances, though vitally
connected with them, the greater part of the catholic
community suffered from a sense of nationalist frustration.
From being part of the national majority in Ireland they
had been forced by partition to become the minority in
Northern Ireland; and of this they did not cease to be
conscious. However they might in practice resign themselves to the new regime, their sense of national identity
remained, and created a mental conflict between their
citizenship of the state in which they found themselves
and their aspiration to belong to a reunited Ireland.
This conflict was both a cause and an effect of those
unionist attitudes and practices which made catholics
feel that they were only second-class citizens in Northern
Ireland. The fact that they enjoyed social and economic
benefits through being within the United Kingdom which
they would not have had in the Republic did not reconcile
them to Northern Ireland, any more than the benefits of
the union before 1921 had converted the catholic body
in Ireland as a whole to unionism. Had it been otherwise,
Northern Ireland would doubtless have succeeded in
achieving political stability and the Irish Republic might
have relinquished its claim to the Six Counties as part of
the national territory. As it was, Northern Ireland
achieved neither political stability nor a satisfactory
political relationship with the rest of Ireland, which has
never recognised Northern Ireland's constitution.

The policy of successive governments in Dublin towards
Northern Ireland till recently was unrealistic, equivocal,
and fluctuating. Mr de Valera, in the course of the treaty
debates in Dáil Éireann (which are largely silent on the
subject of partition), had made the point in a private
session on 22 August 1921 that Ulster had the same justifi-

cation for opting out of an Irish republic that Ireland had for opting out of the United Kingdom. 'For his part, if the Republic were recognised, he would be in favour of giving each county power to vote itself out of the Republic if it so wished.'[1] But this principle was not pursued by the Irish Free State that emerged from the Anglo-Irish treaty of December 1921. Nor was the idea of a 'council of Ireland' for which provision had been made in the Government of Ireland Act 1920 (the legal foundation of partition). This act contemplated· a council, composed of equal numbers of representatives elected by the parliaments of Northern Ireland and Southern Ireland, to initiate proposals for united action between the two and prepare the way for their eventual reunion within the United Kingdom. The parliament of Northern Ireland at once elected its representatives for this purpose (June 1921). But the parliament contemplated for Southern Ireland never came into effect, and the Irish Free State did nothing about the proposed council of Ireland. On the other hand, in 1925, after an unsuccessful attempt to bring about a mutually acceptable adjustment of the boundary between the two areas, the Irish government under W. T. Cosgrave entered into an agreement with the British and Northern Ireland governments, which confirmed the existing boundary, released the Irish Free State from its obligation to bear a share of the public debt of the United Kingdom, and provided for the abandonment of the council of Ireland. In place of the council it was agreed that, to maintain good-neighbour relations, the two Irish governments should meet together whenever necessary to consult about matters of common interest. Nothing, however, came of this hopeful formula, and forty years were to pass before the heads of the Dublin and Belfast governments were to meet again. Mr de Valera's new constitution of 1937 declared the national territory to be the entire island and thus denied the legitimacy of Northern Ireland. Yet, only a year later, in October 1938, Mr de Valera proposed in effect to recognise Northern Ireland on the basis of a 'federal' relationship: he was willing, he said, that Northern Ireland should retain its parliament, its existing powers and its existing area, on condition that fair treatment were guaranteed to the minority and that Northern Ireland would transfer to an all-Ireland parliament the powers that had been reserved

[1]*Private sessions of second dáil* (Dublin, 1973), pp. 28-9.

to the parliament of the United Kingdom under the Government of Ireland Act 1920. Experience of working together on these lines would soon dispel prejudices and prepare the way for the unification of Ireland under a single parliament. Lord Craigavon's response was 'no surrender'; but Mr de Valera and his party thereafter adhered to the idea of a 'federal' arrangement as a principle of settlement.

The neutrality of Ireland and the participation of Northern Ireland in World War II underlined the divergence between south and north. Though it is probable that a majority in the south morally supported the allies in their struggle against Hitler's Germany, and though many thousands of southern Irishmen served in the British forces as volunteers, Mr de Valera had solid popular backing when he insisted, even against pressure from the U.S.A., that Ireland as a state must remain neutral. The principal reason offered was that an Ireland partitioned by Britain could not without forfeiting its own claim to national unity join Britain in a war for democracy and national self-determination. He protested against the arrival of American troops in Northern Ireland in January 1942 on the ground that the maintenance of partition was 'an aggression which his government would denounce, no matter what troops occupied the Six Counties'. Yet it was symbolic of his positive concern for the north that, on the night of a heavy incendiary air-raid on Belfast (15-16 April 1941), he authorised the fire brigades of Dublin, Dun Laoghaire and other towns to rush north to join in fighting the flames.

Britain's acceptance of Ireland's neutrality in World War II, however precarious at times, was the most effective proof of Ireland's sovereignty. This in itself underlined the divergence between north and south, which reached a peak in 1949 when Ireland declared itself to be a republic, and the British parliament affirmed that Northern Ireland was part of the United Kingdom and should not cease to be so without the consent of its parliament. The creation of an 'All-party Anti-partition Conference' in January 1949 by the inter-party government of Mr John A. Costello, and the intensive propaganda-campaign that resulted from it, still further antagonised the majority in Northern Ireland.

Though reunion by peaceful means was proclaimed by successive Irish governments to be one of two great unfulfilled national aims, little was done positively to promote unity, and the attempt to revive the Irish language, the other great national aim, was pursued in a way certain to drive Ulster unionists further than ever from nationalism. Social policies in the south in such matters as censorship, the absence of provision for divorce, and the prohibition on the sale of contraceptives were regarded as proof that the Irish Republic was dominated by the catholic church. A theory generally current in the south was that Britain was wholly responsible for partition and that, if the British garrison could be got out of Northern Ireland, Ulster protestants would enter into fraternal union with the rest of Ireland, probably on a federal basis. But most people in the south, while always prepared to make appropriate ritual noises, were inclined to accept Northern Ireland as a fact, and to have no active interest in its problems or in reunification. Not so the I.R.A., which, continuing the tradition of revolutionary nationalism that self-government had made an anachronism in the south, maintained intermittent guerilla activities against government in Northern Ireland and in Britain. This in turn helped to justify the unionist argument that catholics were enemies of the state, even though catholics in Northern Ireland did not in general support the I.R.A. The fact that the I.R.A. operated from bases in the south was seen as evidence that the Dublin government, though openly renouncing the use of force against Northern Ireland, secretly approved of it. Yet the I.R.A. was an illegal organisation in the south as well as the north, and during its campaign of 1956-62 the Dublin government interned over 100 of its members.

Despite such divergences between the Irish Republic and Northern Ireland practical cooperation did take place on an administrative level, as in the Erne drainage and hydro-electricity scheme, the Foyle fisheries commission, and the rescue of the Great Northern Railway. This policy was dramatically developed by Mr de Valera's successor as taoiseach, Mr Sean Lemass (1959-66), for many years minister for industry and commerce, whose energy, realism and pragmatic genius were at last given full scope, and who led the Republic into a phase of great economic expansion. His acceptance of an invitation from Captain O'Neill to visit him led to two historic meetings, one in Belfast (14 January 1965) and one in Dublin (9 February); they were the first since 1925 to be held between prime ministers of the two Irelands, and they seemed to open a new era of genuine understanding, cooperation and good neighbourliness. An immediate consequence of the exchange of visits was that, for the first time, the nationalist M.P.s in the Stormont parliament decided to act as the official opposition, under the leadership of Mr Eddie McAteer. The fiftieth anniversary of the Easter rising in April 1966, when the official commemorations throughout the Republic were paralleled by three weeks of celebrations in the catholic streets of Belfast, created serious embarrassments for Captain O'Neill. Nevertheless the years following his meetings with Mr Lemass seemed the most hopeful in the whole history of north-south relations till the violence of 1968-9 confronted both north and south with the excruciating realities of a northern situation no less unstable, and much more menacing, than it had been when the government of Northern Ireland was set up, fifty years before.

What began as a civil rights movement erupting into sectarian conflict between the aggrieved minority and the apprehensive majority quickly merged into a conflict not over questions of social justice and reform within Northern Ireland but over the issue of the very existence of Northern Ireland, threatened more seriously than ever before by the forces of revolutionary nationalism in the name of an all-Ireland republic.

## VIII

## CONTINUING CRISIS IN NORTHERN IRELAND

The events of the past four years in Northern Ireland are perilous ground for a historian, but some attempt needs to be made to identify the major factors in a shifting, murky, and infinitely complicated situation.

### 1 British intervention

The efforts of the Northern Ireland government under Captain O'Neill's two successors, Major Chichester-Clark (April 1969-March 1971) and Mr Faulkner (March 1971-March 1972), to make Stormont rule acceptable to the catholics were frustrated by the hostility of unionist extremists on the one hand and of nationalist extremists on the other. The continuance of the communal violence, in its beginnings essentially spontaneous and unconcerted,[1] caused a momentous change in British policy towards Northern Ireland. Hitherto the British government had left the unionist party to rule Northern Ireland with virtually no interference; but when on 14 August 1969 the British prime minister, Mr Harold Wilson, and his home secretary, Mr James Callaghan, made their fateful decision to comply with the Northern Ireland government's appeal for the use of British troops to restore order, they were well aware that they were undertaking responsibilities that might result in the suspension of Stormont itself. The G.O.C. (Northern Ireland) was given exclusive responsibility for all security operations in Northern Ireland, with full control over the R.U.C. and the 'B Specials' in

[1]*Violence and civil disturbances in Northern Ireland in 1969* (the Scarman report—Belfast: H.M.S.O., 1972), i, 11.

the field of security; a senior British official was appointed United Kingdom representative in Northern Ireland; and Mr Callaghan already had contingency plans drawn up to provide for the direct government of Northern Ireland from London.[2] On 15 August troops moved into Derry and Belfast; and from a strength of about 3,000 at that point, the British army in Northern Ireland rose to about 13,000 in July 1970, to about 14,000 in July 1971, and to about 21,000 in July 1972.[3] At the same time British initiative brought about the disarming, civilianisation and reorganisation of the R.U.C., the disbandment of the 'B Specials', and the formation of the Ulster Defence Regiment under British-army control. But neither the reorganised police nor the troops were able to control the violence.

The troops, who had been welcomed as deliverers, within a year had come to be regarded by catholics as brutal partizans of the Stormont government; and this in turn brought the I.R.A. into action in the role of defenders of the catholics against British military 'brutalities'. Brutalities there were, especially in the searches for arms in catholic areas, and few searches were made in protestant areas. But the troops had an almost impossible task, which in general they tackled with patience and restraint, often in face of extreme provocation. This made the occasional lurid incident all the more egregious, and as such incidents grew more frequent the troops acquired a reputation for ruthlessness which their general behaviour did not warrant. The hardening of the army's attitude from July 1970 onwards was believed among catholics to spring from the change of government in Britain in June, when a general election brought Mr Edward Heath and the conservatives to power in place of Mr Wilson and the labour party. But though historically labour has shown more sensitivity to the Irish question than the conservative party, the behaviour of the conservatives in the present Ulster crisis has conspicuously departed from the precedents of 1886, 1893, and 1912-14, when they were in open alliance with militant protestantism in Ulster to defeat Gladstonian home-rule for Ireland. In the present crisis the continuity between the Ulster policy of Mr

[2]James Callaghan, *A house divided: the dilemma of Northern Ireland* (London, 1973), pp 20-23, 41-4.
[3]*The future of Northern Ireland: a paper for discussion* (London: H.M.S.O., 1972), pp 30-31.

Wilson and of Mr Heath is more significant than the contrast. Mr Wilson brought the army into the Northern Ireland situation as the lesser evil, and Mr Heath has kept it there for the same reason and against mounting pressure in England for its recall. On the other hand it appears that Mr Heath's home secretary, Mr Reginald Maudling, allowed more freedom of action to the northern government and the men on the ground than Mr Callaghan had done, and that in consequence the change of government had a worsening effect on the course of events.[4] Continued fighting between the I.R.A. and the security forces, and mounting communal violence, caused Mr Faulkner's government, after consultation with the British government, to resort to the weapon of internment on a large scale against the I.R.A. (August 1971). This in turn intensified the embitterment and alienation of the catholic population in general. In the end, as Mr Callaghan had foreseen, the British government found itself obliged to assume direct responsibility for the government of Northern Ireland. Mr Faulkner and his cabinet were compelled to resign, the Stormont parliament was suspended, and a temporary administration was set up under Mr William Whitelaw as secretary of state for Northern Ireland (March 1972).

Though direct rule was accompanied by worse fighting than ever, Mr Whitelaw initiated a flood of consultation and discussion, and elicited suggestions for the future of Northern Ireland from a wide spectrum of interests, including some 2,500 individual citizens. In August 1972 he invited spokesmen of all the seven political parties that had been represented in the Northern Ireland house of commons[5] to meet in conference at Darlington (County Durham) to discuss possibilities of settlement. The Nationalist Party, the Republican Labour Party, and the Social Democratic and Labour Party, together representing the catholic community, and the extreme protestant Democratic Unionist Party, declined the invitation; and the conference, which met on 25-7 September, was attended only by representatives of the Ulster Unionist Party, the Alliance Party, and the Northern Ireland Labour Party. The three attending parties, and also the Ulster Liberal Party and the New Ulster Movement submitted proposals to Mr Whitelaw, and the Social

[4]See also below, p. 67.
[5]See p. 55.

Democratic and Labour Party published its own scheme.[6] The outcome of all this mobilisation of opinion was Mr Whitelaw's green paper, *The future of Northern Ireland: a paper for discussion* (October 1972), remarkable alike for its restraint, its insight, its informativeness, its flexible approach, its brevity and its readability. It reviewed the proposals put forward, sought to identify the 'unalterable facts' of the situation, and laid down the vital conditions which, in the view of the British government, any settlement would have to satisfy. These were:

(a) Northern Ireland must remain part of the United Kingdom as long as that is the wish of the majority of the people, but this is not to preclude taking account of the 'Irish dimension' of the problem.

(b) As long as Northern Ireland remains part of the United Kingdom, the British government must have 'an effective and continuing voice in Northern Ireland's affairs', commensurate with its economic and military commitment in the province.

(c) Ambiguity in the relationship between the British government and any regional government in Northern Ireland must be avoided.

(d) The primary purposes of any new institutions for Northern Ireland must be (i) 'to seek a much wider consensus than has hitherto existed', and (ii) to be such as will work efficiently and be capable of achieving peace and order, physical development, and social and economic progress. 'Northern Ireland's problems flow not just from a clash of national aspirations or from friction between the communities, but also from social and economic conditions such as inadequate housing and unemployment.'

(e) Any new institutions must be simple and businesslike, and 'appropriate to the powers and functions of a regional authority'.

(f) A Northern Ireland assembly must be capable of involving all its members constructively so that they and their constituents are satisfied that the whole community has a real part to play in the government of the province. There are strong

[6]The proposals of all these groups are printed in *The future of Northern Ireland: a paper for discussion* (London: H.M.S.O., 1972).

arguments for believing that such participation should be achieved by giving the minority a share in the exercise of executive power.

(g)   An assurance that there will be absolute fairness and equality of opportunity for all must be built into any new structure.

(h)   Future arrangements for security and public order must command public confidence both in Northern Ireland and in the United Kingdom as a whole. 'In the present situation, where the army and the police are both involved in maintaining law and order and combating terrorism, it is essential that there should be a single source of direct responsibility. Since Westminister alone can control the armed forces of the crown this unified control must mean Westminster control. For the future any arrangements must ensure that the United Kingdom government has an effective and determining voice in relation to any circumstances which involve, or may involve in the future, the commitment of the armed forces, the use of emergency powers, or repercussions at international level.[7]

On the basis of these conditions the British government went on to produce a white paper, *Northern Ireland constitutional proposals* (March 1973), which laid down a plan for the ending of direct rule and the restoration of regional autonomy. The plan contemplated the election of a new assembly by proportional representation; the development by that assembly of its own rules and procedures; discussion between representatives of the assembly and the secretary of state leading to the formation of an executive; the devolution to the assembly of extensive powers, excluding among other matters control over the security forces, the appointment and removal of judges, parliamentary and local authority elections, special powers for dealing with terrorism, and, for the present, control over the police. A committee system, 'designed to create a strong link between the assembly and the executive' and 'to involve majority and minority interests alike in constructive work' was to be established. Each political head of a government department would act as chairman of a committee, whose membership would reflect the balance of parties in the assembly, and the committee chairmen

[7]Ibid., pp 35-6.

would collectively form the executive of Northern Ireland. Provision would be made, including the setting-up of a standing advisory commission on human rights, to prevent discrimination on the ground of religious belief or political opinion, and to facilitate the establishment of institutional arrangements for consultation and cooperation between Northern Ireland and the Irish Republic. To enable the people of Northern Ireland to declare their views on the border issue periodic plebiscites would be held. The former parliament of Northern Ireland would be abolished, and so would the office of governor, but there would continue to be a secretary of state for Northern Ireland, who would be a member of the British cabinet. This programme was duly embodied in the Northern Ireland Constitution Act 1973, which became law on 18 July. The new constitution meant a considerable diminution of autonomy as compared with the constitution before direct rule, but still gave Northern Ireland a greater degree of self-government than any other part of the United Kingdom. Moreover it was clearly implied that control over the police and other reserved powers would be restored to a Northern Ireland government when 'the present security situation' had changed.

The first local-government elections under the new structure of district councils[8] were held on 30 May 1973. They were the first local elections in Northern Ireland since 1967, the first to which the 'one man one vote' principle applied, the first since 1920 in which there were contests in all areas, and the first local elections in Northern Ireland to be conducted under P.R. The new system worked smoothly and there was a 68% poll, but voting seems generally to have polarised on the protestant-catholic, unionist-nationalist issues, and the outcome broadly conformed to the traditional pattern of party distribution. Unionists—though there was some confusion between official and non-official candidates—gained an absolute majority in ten of the twenty-six districts, and 'loyalists' in one district. The anti-unionist parties did not obtain a majority in any district but formed the largest group in four—Derry, Magherafelt, Mourne and Newry. Of the total of 526 seats in the councils as a whole, over 200 went to unionists and about 70 to 'loyalists'. The new Social Democratic and Labour Party (S.D.L.P.)[9] emerged

[8]See above, pp 39-40.
[9]See below, pp 75-8.

as the main opposition group with about 80 seats. The Northern Ireland Labour Party was almost eliminated, and the new centre group, the Alliance Party[10], won about 60 seats. No other party won as many as 20 seats. In several districts Republican Club and Unity candidates (representing the Official and the Provisional I.R.A.[11] respectively) contested seats with the S.D.L.P., but their total successes were numerically insignificant. It was generally supposed that this voting pattern prefigured the probable outcome of the impending elections to the new assembly.

These elections were held in accordance with the provisions of a separate act (the Northern Ireland Assembly Act 1973) on 28 June, with the following result:

*Membership of the N.I. assembly, 1973*

|  | nos | % |
|---|---|---|
| Official unionists | 23 | |
| Alliance Party | 8 | |
| Northern Ireland Labour Party | 1 | |
| Pro-assembly unionists | 32 | 41 |
| Unpledged unionists | 10 | |
| Vanguard Unionist Progressive Party | 7 | |
| Democratic Unionist Party | 8 | |
| West Belfast Loyalist Coalition | 2 | |
| Dissident unionists | 27 | 37 |
| Total unionists | 59 | 76 |
| Social Democratic and Labour Party | 19 | 24 |
| Total membership | 78 | 100 |

As compared with the results of the local elections, the elections for the assembly show a large increase in the total proportion of unionists, but this is offset by the

[10]See below, pp 77-8.
[11]See below, pp 66, 72.

sharp division between pro-assembly and dissident unionists. The pro-assembly unionists outnumber the dissidents by a narrow margin, and this only with the support of the Alliance Party. Both the Alliance Party and the S.D.L.P. have suffered proportional losses as compared with their showing in the local elections. The membership of the new assembly may be compared with the membership of the suspended house of commons as follows:

*Membership of the N.I. house of commons, 1972*

|  | nos | % |
|---|---|---|
| Official unionists | 32 | |
| Democratic Unionist Party | 4 | |
| Alliance Party | 3 | |
| Northern Ireland Labour Party | 1 | |
| Independent | 1 | |
| Unionists | 41 | 79 |
| Social Democratic and Labour Party | 6 | |
| Nationalists | 4 | |
| Republican Labour Party | 1 | |
| Nationalists | 11 | 21 |
| Total membership | 52 | 100 |

The most significant change in the composition of the two assemblies is two-fold. (1) The percentage of unionists has decreased marginally, from 79% to 76%, but these unionists are split fairly evenly between supporters and opponents of the new assembly. The pro-assembly unionists are broadly committed to the principle of power-sharing in accordance with the Northern Ireland Constitution Act 1973, the dissident unionists either are not pledged to this official unionist policy or are openly bent on wrecking the assembly and stultifying the act. The pro-assembly unionists comprise: (a) official unionists under the leadership of Mr Faulkner, a group that is the largest in the assembly but includes members whose allegiance to Mr Faulkner's policy is not wholly to be relied on; (b) the Alliance Party, solidly pro-assembly under its chairman Mr Oliver Napier; and (c) Mr David Bleakley, formerly minister of community relations, the sole member of the Northern Ireland Labour Party to win a seat in the assembly, of which he is a firm supporter. The dissident unionists[12] consist of: (a) unpledged unionists, chief among whom are Mr John Taylor and Mr Harry West, (b) Mr Craig's Vanguard Unionist Progressive Party, and (c) the Democratic Unionist Party led by Rev. Ian Paisley, together with two members from the West Belfast Loyalist Coalition. All the dissidents demand the restoration of the former Stormont parliament with unimpaired powers and no 'capitulation to republicanism'. (2) The percentage of nationalists has increased marginally, from 21% to 24%, but in place of three groups there is now only one, the S.D.L.P., which could thus have a decisive role in the new assembly. At all events, for the first time in the parliamentary history of Northern Ireland, the unionist-nationalist polarisation has been superseded by a complex system of political forces, in which there might emerge an executive supported by moderate unionists and nationalists and an opposition comprising several groups of protestant extremists.

On the other hand, the spectacular failure of the Northern Ireland Labour Party, which was able to return only one of its eighteen candidates to the new assembly, followed a familiar pattern: in the twelve general elections in Northern Ireland between 1921 and 1969 the number of successful labour candidates never exceeded four, and in three general elections (1921, 1949 and 1953) was nil. The fact that a labour party as such commands so little support among the electors is an illuminating comment on the anomalous social development of an area that has long been the most industrialised in Ireland.

If the new assembly does not become the starting-point for a real effort in self-government on a basis of equality of citizenship and power-sharing it will not be the fault of Mr Whitelaw, who is the first British statesman to have committed himself fully, and on the spot, to grappling with the problems which have created, and have been created by, partition. His task is the more baffling because, in addition to the conflicting aims and pressures underlying the party alignments in the new assembly, he has had to cope with the continued guerilla campaign of the I.R.A. on the one hand and the counter-violence of protestant extremists on the other, which together have made the

[12]See below, pp 57-65.

period of direct rule the blackest since the present troubles began. To him and his colleagues at Westminster, as to the protestant community in Northern Ireland, the I.R.A. is a monstrous conspiracy against the state and the whole fabric of civilised living, but they are in no doubt that a military victory over the I.R.A. would not in itself lead to a settlement. While the British army tries to contain the violence, Mr Whitelaw seeks to rally all the moderate and responsible elements in Northern Ireland, catholic and protestant, behind his plan for a settlement on a parliamentary basis.

## 2   Unionist disintegration

One of the most momentous changes of the past five years has been the disintegration of the monolithic solidarity that had characterised the unionists since the foundation of Northern Ireland. The process, which began as a reaction against Captain O'Neill's modest reforms, was high-lighted by his dismissal of Mr Craig in December 1968. Since then a tendency to fission has become more characteristic of unionists than unity. The first and primary split was between those who were prepared to make such concessions to catholic demands as seemed to be necessary in order to restore peace and maintain Northern Ireland as an autonomous unit under unionist control within the United Kingdom, and those who, condemning the policy of reform as mere appeasement, were bent on maintaining protestant ascendancy in Northern Ireland at almost any price. Mr Faulkner is the principal leader in the first category, Mr Craig in the second. Each category, but especially the second, has its sub-divisions, so that there are four main unionist groups in the new assembly and many more outside it.

In remaining head of the official unionist party, even after the introduction of direct rule had seemed to cut the ground from under his feet, Mr Faulkner has shown exemplary coolness, skill, tenacity and resilience. He is clearly indispensable to the formation of any power-sharing executive, but the further he moves in the direction of power-sharing and a council of Ireland the less support he is likely to receive from the unionist party. This applies especially to the Ulster Unionist Council, the huge general assembly (nearly 1000 strong) of Ulster unionism,

57

composed of representatives of the local unionist associations, the Orange lodges and other unionist bodies, of unionist members both of the Westminster and Stormont parliaments, and of a large number of coopted members. In this Ulster Unionist Council, whose standing committee appoints, and can depose, the leader of the unionist party, the unpledged unionists are likely to count for proportionately much more than their percentage of members in the assembly. Yet Mr Faulkner can claim that he is a better and more progressive interpreter of unionism than his unionist opponents. Keeping strictly within the field of constitutional action, he has constantly insisted both on the constitutional rights of Northern Ireland and on the vital importance of the British connection. Mr Craig, on the other hand, in championing the claims of the protestant majority has repeatedly expressed his readiness to resort to force in certain circumstances not specified, and has repeatedly used the threat of U.D.I. (Unilateral Declaration of Independence), or self-determination for Northern Ireland on the precedent of Mr Ian Smith's Rhodesia. Like nearly all unionist politicians, both Mr Faulkner and Mr Craig belong to the Orange Order, which remains the fullest expression of traditional protestant solidarity. But the influence of the Order on the course of events has become much less than that of new and more ruthless para-military organisations of protestant extremists, responding in kind to the violence of the I.R.A. Mr Craig has identified himself somewhat equivocally with this 'protestant backlash',[13] especially through his 'Ulster Vanguard', an umbrella organisation of loyalist militants launched in February 1972, which includes large numbers of former 'B Specials'. On 18 March, at a mammoth Vanguard rally in the Ormeau Park, Belfast, he promised that a provisional government for Northern Ireland would be set up if the British government attempted to impose a new constitution on the loyalist majority against its will; and he added: 'we must build up the dossier on those men and women in this country who are a menace to this country, because, . . . if and when the politicians fail us, it may be our job to liquidate the enemy'.[14] But Vanguard's retort to direct rule went no further than a two-day strike (27-8 March) of almost the entire protestant work-force,

[13]See below, pp 72-5.
[14]Quoted in David Boulton, *The U. V. F. 1966-73: an anatomy of loyalist rebellion* (Dublin, 1973), p. 156.

culminating in a mass rally at Stormont at which Mr Faulkner himself appeared on the platform. It might have seemed as if Mr Faulkner was ready to join with Mr Craig in an updated version of the unionist 'rebellion' of 1912-14. But however deeply he resented the suspension of Stormont, Mr Faulkner was too much of a realist to commit himself to Mr Craig's position; and the membership of the new assembly reflects the division that now seems to have set firm between unionists who follow Mr Faulkner and those who follow Mr Craig.

Among official unionists, one of Mr Faulkner's principal colleagues, Mr Roy Bradford, who was successively minister of commerce (1969-71) and minister of development (1971-2), has emerged as the exponent of a new style in unionist politics: urbane, outward-looking and progressive, conciliatory but firm in his approach to political opponents and perceptive in his attitude to the Republic, he would appear to be cast for a leading role in the new assembly. Among unionist dissidents in the assembly a no less distinctive figure is Mr John Taylor, who was minister of state for home affairs (1970-72) and the victim of an assassination attempt by the Official I.R.A. (26 February 1972). At the Aughnacloy Orange demonstration of 12 July 1972 he warned his hearers that British policy was neither to defeat the I.R.A. nor to strengthen the union between Britain and Northern Ireland, and that this called for painful rethinking by loyalists, many of whose beliefs, traditions and sympathies would have to be abandoned. He has declared that his ambition is 'to experience mutual respect and cooperation between Ulster and the Republic of Ireland'.[15]

A disruptive element within unionism that it is hard to assess has for many years been forming round the massive personality of Rev. Ian Paisley, who combines the role of fundamentalist preacher and leader of a small but growing evangelical sect (the Free Presbyterian Church, founded by himself in 1951), with that of tough, stentorian and resourceful demagogue and astute, flexible and quick-witted politician. With a gift for repartee, the pungent phrase and the humorous quip, and with a disarming smile, he has become expert in the use of the mass media, especially television. A blood-curdling spokesman of those atavistic fears of 'Romanism' that still haunt

[15]*Who's who, what's what and where in Ireland* (London and Dublin. 1973). p. 622.

many Ulster protestants, he first earned notoriety in 1956 by his association with the case of Maura Lyons, a fifteen-year old catholic girl who, having become a convert to protestantism through his preaching, and having in consequence encountered parental opposition, mysteriously disappeared. She remained in hiding for over six months till May 1957 when, on reaching the age of sixteen, she presented herself at Mr Paisley's home to ask for his protection. He notified the police, who placed her in a remand centre pending legal proceedings. On a petition on behalf of her parents to have her made a ward of court, the case came before the lord chief justice, Lord MacDermott. He granted the petition, severely censuring those responsible for the abduction, appointing the girl's father as her guardian, and forbidding Mr Paisley, who had declined to give evidence, to have access to her (20 May 1957). She was restored to her family and eventually returned to the church she had renounced.

Mr Paisley's activities against the catholic church continued, and in October 1962 he appeared in Rome for the opening of Pope John XXIII's Vatican Council to protest against the presence of protestant observers in that epoch-making assembly. Regarding ecumenism as an insidious attempt to undo the protestant reformation, he went on to link it in his denunciations with the reforming policy of official unionism as interpreted by Captain O'Neill. He became the unbridled critic of Captain O'Neill as a weak-kneed, upper-class unionist, totally unfit to lead the protestant people of Ulster. In 1966 he founded the Ulster Constitution Defence Committee and Ulster Protestant Volunteers (U.P.V.) a 'united society of protestant patriots pledged by all lawful methods to uphold and maintain the constitution of Northern Ireland as an integral part of the United Kingdom so long as the United Kingdom maintains a protestant monarchy and the terms of the revolution settlement'.[16] He and his colleague, Major Ronald Bunting, commandant of the U.P.V., were prominently identified with the protestant violence mounted against the civil rights marchers of 1968-9; and the Cameron commission attributed to them and their organisation a heavy share of direct responsibility for the disorders in Armagh and at Burntollet Bridge, and also for inflaming passions and engineering opposition to lawful, and what would in all probability have been peaceful,

[16]*Cameron report*, p. 118.

demonstrations'.[17] Prosecuted for taking part in an unlawful assembly at Armagh on 30 November, they were both found guilty and sentenced to three months imprisonment by the Armagh magistrates, who ordered that at the expiration of their sentences they should be bound in recognisances of £100 to be of good behaviour for two years, or in default should serve a further month in prison (27 January 1969). They appealed against the sentence, and were offered release by a county court judge on condition of being bound over to keep the peace, which they refused. The judge therefore confirmed their prison sentences, and increased the amount of the recognisances in the magistrates' order to £250, and the period of further imprisonment in default of being bound over to three months (25 March). In fact they gained the halo that imprisonment alone could give after serving less than two months in Belfast jail, being released in May under an amnesty declared by the new prime minister, Major Chichester-Clark, for all persons imprisoned or awaiting trial in connection with the civil rights demonstrations.

Mr Paisley had already turned his attention to the parliamentary field, and in the general election of February 1969 had challenged, and come near to defeating, Captain O'Neill in the prime minister's own constituency of Bannside. In April 1970 he captured this constituency at a by-election, and in the United Kingdom general election of June 1970 he also won a seat at Westminster. In his double capacity as M.P. he played down the character of demagogue and played up that of man of peace and moderation, while competing with Mr Craig for the leadership of the 'loyalists' in opposition to official unionism under Mr Faulkner. With Mr Desmond Boal, Q.C., M.P., who had become his political ally as well as his legal adviser, he founded in September 1971 the Democratic Unionist Party, described by Mr Boal as 'right-wing in the sense of being strong on the constitution and restoring security, but to the left on social policies'.[18] With a strength of four (themselves, Rev. William Beattie, and Mr John McQuade) in the Stormont parliament the new party declared itself, on the withdrawal of the nationalists, to be the official opposition. Mr Paisley now seemed to be heading for a new kind of unionism, radically different from that of both Mr Faulkner and Mr Craig in seek-

[17]Ibid., pp 89-90.
[18]Quoted in Boulton, *The U.V.F.*, p. 142.

ing to base itself not on the traditional protestant combination of classes but on the protestant working classes. He and his perceptive colleague seemed well aware that such a new departure might lead to the transcending of sectarian division between protestant and catholic workers. They found themselves in agreement with the new left-wing nationalist combination, the Social Democratic and Labour Party,[19] on the urgent need to reduce employment by large-scale state intervention, and in attacking Mr Faulkner over internment, which they saw as a weapon that might be turned against the Democratic Unionists. And Mr Boal went so far as to condemn the Orange Order, the most sacred institution of traditional unionism:

How can we complain about the sinister influence of the Roman Catholic Church in the political and social life of the republic when we ourselves are vulnerable to the charge that direct representation of the Orange Order in the government party may arouse in Roman Catholics a corresponding fear that what is to them just as malign an influence exists in the bodies that decide policy in this country?[20]

On 25 November 1971, commenting on a plan of settlement proposed by Mr Harold Wilson, Mr Paisley made an astonishing gesture to the Republic. The great obstacle to Irish unity, he said, was the special position conceded to the catholic church in the Irish constitution. If this were altered, and if protestants could be sure that the catholic church could no longer dictate to the Dublin government, 'then there would be a new set of circumstances, where there could be good neighbourliness in the highest possible sense'.[21] The sensational change of front that this seemed to imply was welcomed both by a senior member of the Dublin government and by a leading spokesman of the Provos, and Mr Faulkner lost no time in describing Mr Paisley as 'the darling of the republican press'. A grassroots reaction against him set in which he hastily sought to counter by a protestation on 9 December that he was absolutely opposed to any kind of united Ireland.

He and Mr Boal fiercely attacked the new Vanguard movement, and exposed the contradiction between Mr

[19]See below, pp 75-7.
[20]Quoted in Boulton, *The U.V.F.*, pp 147-8.
[21]Quoted ibid.. p. 148.

Craig's threats of U.D.I. and his professions of unionist loyalty. Convinced that direct rule was imminent, Mr Paisley declared that, rather than patch up a Stormont that had demonstrably failed, it would be better to integrate Northern Ireland completely in the United Kingdom, at the same time increasing its representation at Westminster. This maverick pronouncement caused further confusion in the loyalist ranks, but gave its author temporarily a better claim to moderation than Mr Faulkner, who had predicted catastrophe if the Stormont parliament were abolished. Paradoxically it also enabled Mr Paisley to avoid the charge of inconsistency when, a year later, he joined forces with his former rival in a campaign to stultify Mr Whitelaw's plan for a new assembly, which Mr Faulkner was now preparing to make the best of. In November 1972 Mr Craig announced a new right-wing party, the Vanguard Unionist Progressive Party, which, in conjunction with Mr Paisley's Democratic Unionist Party, would challenge official unionism at the forthcoming elections both for the local councils and for the new assembly. The outcome has not been very gratifying to either Mr Craig or Mr Paisley, with a party of 7 and 8 respectively in an assembly of 78. In the light of Mr Paisley's bewildering changes of alignment since 1966, his future political action is especially unpredictable, but it would seem that his bid for the leadership of a new working-class unionist movement has failed.

Subsidiary to the main split in unionism are other splits arising out of (1) working-class dissatisfaction with traditional unionist leadership as both ineffective against the I.R.A. and as out of touch with the real needs of the working-class, and (2) a widespread sense among loyalists of being betrayed by Britain, whose interests these loyalists have maintained in Ireland so faithfully for so long.

The first of these subsidiary sources of division helps to explain both working-class support for, and controversy with, Mr Craig's Vanguard movement, and also a tendency for working-class protestant militants to look beyond the religious divide and see their interests in a wider context. An early example of this was the foundation, in March 1969, of the Workers' Committee for the Defence of the Constitution by Mr Billy Hull, a leading shopsteward in Harland and Wolff's shipyard and known as 'the unofficial mayor of the Shankill'. His newspaper, *People's Press,* announced:

The ordinary working people are the backbone of the United Kingdom, and this applies as much to Northern Ireland as to England, Scotland and Wales. The children of the workers deserve the opportunity of higher education, and . . . they are not getting it here to-day. Where there ought to be rows of terraced houses with modern bathrooms, up-to-date playing fields and old people's homes, swimming pools and normal necessities of life today, the Shankill Road and other workers' areas present a bleak picture of desolation. . . . The leaders of unionism have not inherited our automatic support.[22]

The difference between this attitude and the traditional outlook of working-class unionists in some sense paralleled that between the Official and the Provisional I.R.A.[23]

Another protestant militant of the Shankill Road, Mr 'Gusty' Spence, who was serving a life-sentence for the murder of a catholic,[24] wrote from Belfast jail to condole with the widow of the Official I.R.A. leader, Joe McCann, a charismatic figure among Belfast catholics, who was shot dead in the street by a British soldier (15 April 1972). Soon afterwards, at the head of some thirty U.V.F.[24] prisoners, Mr Spence joined with a similar number of Official I.R.A. men in a strike for political status, which eventually succeeded. What followed is almost incredible: though a life-sentenced prisoner, Mr Spence was released on parole for forty-eight hours on 30 June to attend a daughter's wedding, but remained at large, being allegedly held against his will by the U.V.F., for over four months. Under armed guard he gave a press-interview at which he declared that he was not guilty of murder, that his trial had been a farce, that he deplored sectarian assassination, and that the unionist party had got the loyalists of Northern Ireland into 'one hell of a mess'.

One has only to look at the Shankill Road, the heart of the empire, that lies torn and bleeding. We have known squalor. I was born and reared in it. No one knows better than we do the meaning of slums, the meaning of deprivation, the meaning of suffering for what one believes in, whatever the

[22]Quoted in Boulton. *The U.V.F.,* p. 138.
[23]See below, pp 66, 72.
[24]See below. p. 72.

ideology. In so far as people speak of fifty years of misrule, I wouldn't disagree with that. What I would say is this, that we have suffered every bit as much as the people of the Falls Road, or any other underprivileged quarter, in many cases more so.[25]

Here we appear to have a Gusty Spence who, in sharp contrast with the founder of the U.V.F. in 1966, sees working-class protestants and catholics as equally the victims of ascendancy government, and by implication sees the 'protestant backlash' as a kind of irrelevance.

The second of the two subsidiary sources of division among unionists first came into the story when British troops were used to protect catholics against protestant attack, receded when the troops became embroiled with the I.R.A., and revived in full force with the introduction of direct rule and the abolition of Stormont. The sense of being abandoned to their hereditary enemies by Britain for no other reason than excess of 'loyalty' helped to rally protestant extremists around Mr Craig, with his promises of massive loyalist action to maintain 'strong, effective, undiluted majority rule in Ulster'—in other words to prevent, in the name of democracy, any sharing of power with catholics. On the other hand, many unionists who sympathised with this aim were repelled both by Mr Craig's methods and by his talk of secession from the United Kingdom. In the new assembly the Craigites, the Paisleyites and the 'unpledged' unionists seem to have little in common except hostility to the new constitution, whose key-stone is power-sharing.


## 3   The intervention of the I.R.A.

The breach between the British forces and the catholics from April 1970 onwards was both the cause of, and the opportunity for, the intervention of the I.R.A., which had not hitherto played any distinctive part in the fighting, though it had taken an active interest in the civil rights movement. In the role of defenders of victimised catholics they launched an urban guerilla campaign against the British forces and the Northern Ireland government. The British army, which had been brought in primarily to protect catholics against protestant extremists, thus had

[25]Quoted in Boulton, *The U.V.F.*, p. 172.

to take on the task of defeating the I.R.A., which meant that they were involved in hostilities against catholics. The I.R.A. campaign, waged with increasingly sophisticated weapons of war, imported from abroad, has been maintained with varying success for three years during which over 850 people have been killed, innumerable others injured physically and mentally, thousands of working-class people, catholic and protestant, driven from their homes, and a vast amount of property destroyed in Belfast, Derry and elsewhere.

The sectarian fighting of 1969 found the I.R.A. unprepared to take any active part in the defence of the catholics. Since the previous I.R.A. campaign (1956-62) a Marxist element had been endeavouring to convert the organisation from its traditional military role into becoming a base for an advanced left-wing movement on political and social lines. When catholics in Derry and Belfast were under fierce attack from loyalists in August 1969 the I.R.A., lacking arms and organisation, were immobilised: 'I.R.A.—I Ran Away' was chalked up on walls in the beleaguered ghettos. In September the staff of the Belfast brigade reorganised itself and broke away from the official army council; and in December, when an I.R.A. convention in Dublin voted in favour of recognition of the Dublin, Belfast and Westminster governments, the minority seceded and set up a 'provisional army council'. A corresponding split occurred in January 1970 at the convention in Dublin of the I.R.A.'s political front, Sinn Féin. The 'Provisionals'—in the vernacular, 'Provos'—or 'green' republicans were those who followed the example of the Belfast brigade and adhered to the provisional army council; the 'Officials' or 'red' republicans were those who continued to recognise the official army council. Both the Provos and the Officials engaged in the guerilla fighting, but the former, with its own six-county command, based in Belfast, quickly assumed the leadership of the resistance to British authority in Northern Ireland and bore the main brunt of the fighting. For them the one vital issue was the struggle to overthrow that authority and to unite the six counties with the twenty-six in an Irish republic. By February 1971 the Provos were well entrenched in the Ballymurphy, Ardoyne, and New Lodge Road areas of Belfast and in the Bogside and Creggan areas of Derry, while the Officials claimed to be in control of the Lower Falls area of Belfast. These were the barricaded 'no-go' areas, from which the I.R.A. were able to exclude the R.U.C. and where the government's writ ceased to run. The catholics in these areas, all distinctively working-class. were frequently as terrified of the Provos as of the British forces, and longed for peace and order. But while most of them had no wish to see the British forces withdrawn immediately, they could not but see the British troops in the light of intruders, whereas the Provos, however atrocious their actions, were sometimes the only defenders of the catholics and at all times had vital links with the local catholic communities.

A new source of embitterment and complexity was created when on 9 August 1971, following the bloodiest day Belfast and Derry had known since the present violence began, Mr Faulkner invoked the special powers act to arrest and imprison indefinitely without trial several hundred I.R.A. suspects. Internment immediately gave rise to furious and sustained allegations of brutality and torture, especially the use of interrogation 'in depth', inflicted by the police and the army on their prisoners, allegations which an official inquiry (August-November 1971)[26] showed to be substantially justified. A further inquiry (November 1971-January 1972)[27] reviewed the methods of interrogation; and the minority report of one of its three members, Lord Gardiner, who firmly condemned these methods, was at once accepted by the British government. But allegations of ill-treatment continued. Catholics in general have shown bitter hostility to internment, and moderate leaders such as Mr John Hume, of the S.D.L.P., who had been foremost in denouncing the violence of the I.R.A., were no less vehement in demanding the release of the internees. All nationalist M.P.s withdrew from the Stormont parliament, many moderate catholics from public bodies on which they were serving, and the S.D.L.P. launched a civil disobedience campaign involving a strike against rent and rates. Internment and the reaction to it have had the effect of inflicting great suffering on innumerable working-class catholic families, from which nearly all the internees till recently have been drawn. But to most protestants internment has seemed a necessary evil in face of I.R.A. terrorism. Since direct rule was introduced, many internees and detainees have been released, the system itself has

[26]The Compton inquiry; see bibliography, below, p. 121.
[27]The Parker inquiry; see bibliography, below p. 121.

been modified, and its operation has been extended to include protestant suspects; this is no doubt one reason for the increasing protestant criticism that is being directed against it.

The Provos welcomed the 'fall of Stormont' as a signal victory for them, and, while rejecting direct rule as another British threat to Irish independence, negotiated a truce with Mr Whitelaw, which began on 26 June 1972, for the purpose of discussing their three-point peace plan: (1) a British declaration acknowledging the right of the Irish people to self-determination; (2) a commitment by Britain to withdraw her army by a specified date; (3) a general amnesty. A secret meeting was held in London between Mr Whitelaw and a Provo delegation on 7 July; no agreement was reached, and before talks could be resumed the truce was called-off by the Provos on 9 July when the army became involved in conflict between catholics and protestants over the allocation of houses to displaced catholic families at Lenadoon, near Belfast. The Provos renewed their offensive, and Mr Whitelaw replied with 'Operation Motorman' on 31 July, when strong forces of troops supported by tanks moved into, and reoccupied, the 'no-go' areas in Belfast, Derry and else-where—without, however, achieving any decisive result against the Provos.

The actual fighting-men among the Provos have never exceeded some hundreds, and they have suffered severe losses to the British security forces by death and intern-ment. They have increasingly called into active service their women's organisation, Cumann na mBan, and their youth organisation, Fianna na hEireann, recruited from teenagers and children. One of the most tragic and horrifying features of the present troubles is that, in the ghettos of Derry, Belfast and elsewhere, young people, both boys and girls, have become habituated to violence, are themselves engaged in it, and are indoctrinated in the cult of violence. But though pitted against a heavily-armed regular army many times their number, the Provos have advantages, of which they are well aware, common to urban guerillas all over the world. They cannot defeat the British army, but so long as their morale and their local support and their war-supplies hold out they cannot be eliminated except at a cost in civilian lives and property that the British are not prepared to inflict. The car-bomb explosions in the city of London in March 1973 show their readiness and their capacity to carry their war into Britain itself. Outside Northern Ireland they receive active support from members and sympathisers in the Republic, and, to augment the proceeds of bank-robberies both in Northern Ireland and in the Republic, money is forthcoming from Irish republican sources in Britain and abroad, and especially in America, from which for over a century Irish revolutionary organisations have been able to count on financial backing.

The measure of success of the Provos in their war against British authority in Northern Ireland has highlighted one of the weaknesses of partition as an expedient for safeguarding protestant interests. For not only are catholics in a majority west of the Bann, but they are 67% of the population in Derry City, the most sacred spot in protestant mythology, and 27% of the population of Belfast, the heart and stronghold of protestantism. There are 114,300 catholics in Belfast, which is more than their combined total, 100,700, in Tyrone and Fermanagh. And far from regarding themselves in Belfast and other strongly protestant areas in the six counties as interlopers, they feel irrevocably rooted to these areas. The same is broadly true of protestants who are in a minority in local government areas of Northern Ireland west of the Bann. It is the geographical distribution of catholics in Northern Ireland, combined with the impracticability of sealing off the six counties from the rest of Ulster and Ireland, that has made it so difficult for the British army to deal with the Provos.

The Provos see themselves as engaged in a war against Great Britain and against those directly involved in maintaining British authority in Northern Ireland, but not against protestants as such. They are fully committed guerilla fighters, not political thinkers, but there are political thinkers among them, in whose public statements a political theory and a political programme are to be found. In this theory the Provos' campaign is the final and indispensable phase in an eight-centuries' struggle for national liberation. When Britain has been forced to acknowledge Ireland's right to self-determination and has withdrawn her army, the various elements making up the Irish people will settle their differences and establish a new, democratic and socialist Ireland: 'our aim is to make the Irish people masters of their own destinies, controlling all the wealth of the nation, material and spiritual in an independent republic of 32 counties, in which protestants, catholics and dissenters will have equal

69

rights' (Easter message, 1970, from Provisional Army Council). The constitution proposed by the Provos for the new Ireland would have a 'federal' structure, based on provincial parliaments and governments for the four historic provinces, with a 'federal' parliament and government for the whole country. The setting up of a nine-county Ulster parliament, Dáil Uladh, in which protestants would have a working majority, would be the first step towards the establishment of a new governmental system for all Ireland. Under each provincial government there would be regional development councils for economic, social and cultural affairs, and at the base of the whole structure a system of community councils to replace the existing local authorities. A settlement on such lines would, the Provos believe, be the fulfilment of a centuries-long struggle, and the starting point for a new and happier Ireland.

To abandon the struggle now, with victory almost in sight, would be, the Provos believe, to repeat the disaster of 1921 and betray the dead generations from whose sacrifices Ireland derives her long tradition of nationhood. The Provos are therefore unshaken by the denunciations and the pleadings of those who call for an immediate end to the violence, even though they are the great mass of the population, catholic and protestant, and include the clergy of all the principal churches. They believe that, by keeping up the shooting, the bombing and the disruption of social and economic life in Northern Ireland, they can frustrate the security forces, impair their morale and break the will of the British government: the destruction, human and material, the demoralisation and the anguish that their war inflicts on the whole population, though regrettable, are the price that has to be paid to settle accounts with Britain once and for all; and it is, they claim, their constant endeavour to minimise the suffering and the loss involved for civilians. This argument is, of course, addressed to the local catholic communities, especially the catholic 'ghettos' of Belfast and Derry, to which they mostly belong and on which they vitally depend. How far their strength in these areas is due to the loyalty they inspire, and how far to the intimidation they exert, it is impossible to decide. But they continue to receive a substantial though varying measure of communal support, which is rooted in their acceptance as the only ultimate defenders of the catholics against the British army, the R.U.C., and protestant extremists, rather than in

70

enthusiasm for the idea of an all-Ireland republic. Conse-
quently that support varies with the degree to which the
catholics of the ghettos feel themselves to be victimised
or protected by the forces of the state.

As political theorists the Provos are cast in the dogmatic
mould of the physical-force nationalism established by the
Fenians in the later-nineteenth century. Like the Fenians
they have no doubt of their moral right to wage war
against Great Britain. They are infallible interpreters of
the will of the Irish people to achieve independence and
unification, no matter what the cost. They look with great
animosity upon other schools of nationalism—the Official
I.R.A., whose nationalism is permeated with international
socialism; moderate Ulster nationalists, and especially the
S.D.L.P., who seek a non-violent and gradualist settlement
of the national question; the government of the Irish
Republic, which they denounce as corrupt, reactionary,
hypocritical and time-serving; and the majority of the
citizens of the Republic, who support that government.
Towards unionists they have a divided attitude. Moderate
and reforming unionists, especially the official unionist
party, and, above all, the Alliance Party, dedicated to the
idea of an equal partnership of protestants and catholics
in a regenerated Northern Ireland within the United
Kingdom—these they regard with the utmost hostility.
The last thing they wish to see is the success of the
reform-movement. On the other hand they would be very
willing to reach agreement with protestant extremists of
the Craig school, who, in their resentment against reforms
dictated by Britain, are talking loudly of self-determination
for Northern Ireland.

Though they profess to be aiming at a socialist democracy the Provos are essentially nationalists, and they are
deeply and sharply divided from the Officials, who are
essentially Marxian socialists. The Officials accuse the
Provos of fomenting sectarian civil war instead of promoting solidarity among the working classes. The aim of
the Officials is a workers' republic of all Ireland. At
times the hostility between the two groups has erupted
into open fighting, as in Belfast on 10 March 1971. The
Officials have shown themselves on occasion to be no less
ruthless than the Provos—the killing of Senator John
Barnhill in his home on 13 December 1971, and the
bomb-explosion at the officers' mess of the 16th Parachute
Brigade at Aldershot on 23 February 1972, which killed
five cleaning-women, a chaplain and a gardener, are

examples of their work—but differences with the Provos over tactics caused them to declare a limited cease-fire on 29 May 1972, since when their operations have been restricted to what they describe as 'defensive retaliation'.

The counterpart in the political sphere to the I.R.A. in the military is Sinn Féin, which is illegal in Northern Ireland but legal in the Republic. Sinn Féin, like the I.R.A. is split into Provisionals and Officials, each being distinguished by the location of its headquarters in Dublin, the former at Kevin Street, the latter at Gardiner Place. In the general election of 28 February 1973 in the Republic, Sinn Féin (Gardiner Place) ran ten candidates, and in that of 28 July in Northern Ireland the equivalent group there, under the name of Republican Clubs, ran nine candidates. It is some measure of the extent of popular support for Official Sinn Féin that in neither election, on a basis of proportional representation, did the party win a single seat. There is no corresponding way of measuring popular support for the Provos, since they, like orthodox Fenians of the last century, have refused to take any part in parliamentary politics.

## 4   The 'protestant backlash'

As we have seen, the present violence in Northern Ireland began in 1968 with the hostile attentions of protestant extremists to a civil rights movement which was largely catholic and which, though moderate in its demands and non-violent in its methods, was infiltrated with subversive elements. The sectarian disturbances that sprang from this situation brought into action various para-military organisations of militant protestants, of which the first and perhaps the most characteristic was the Ulster Volunteer Force (U.V.F.).[28] This was a secret, working-class army formed in 1966 (the anniversary of the 1916 rising) in the protestant stronghold of the Shankill Road, Belfast, to resist, on the precedent of the U.V.F. of 1913, the 'appeasement' policy of Captain O'Neill's government and to maintain protestant supremacy. The new U.V.F. announced that it was at war with

[28]Mr David Boulton's recent book, *The U.V.F., 1966-73: an anatomy of loyalist rebellion* (Dublin, 1973), is a valuable study of these para-military organisations.

the I.R.A., and found its hero-figure in Mr 'Gusty' Spence, who on 26 June 1966 was found guilty of the murder of a young catholic barman, Peter Ward, in Malvern Street, off the Shankill Road, and sentenced to imprisonment for life by Lord Chief Justice MacDermott. Two days after the murder, Captain O'Neill's government invoked the special powers act to declare the U.V.F. an illegal organisation. But though proscribed it remained in being, and, with other para-military protestant groups, engaged in hostilities against the civil rights marches of 1968-9, in the bombing of water and electricity installations in March and April 1969 which led to Captain O'Neill's resignation, and in the fierce sectarian fighting in Belfast during the summer of 1969 which was accompanied by the burning of working-class homes and the displacement of many working-class families, catholic and protestant. The protestant volunteer forces that had done so much to overthrow Captain O'Neill thus played a major part in creating the conditions in which the government had to call on the help of British troops on 14 August 1969 to restore order.

In seeking to restore order the troops at once became engaged in defending catholic areas against protestant attack, and this in turn quickly involved them in fighting with protestant 'loyalists', as on 7 September, when John McKeague and his Shankill Defence Association (S.D.A.) stoned troops, who replied with C.S. gas. This pattern continued, and was intensified when on 10 October the government published the Hunt report recommending the disarming of the R.U.C. and the disbandment of the 'B Specials'.[29] The S.D.A. declared: 'a day is fast approaching when responsible leaders and associations like ourselves will no longer be able to restrain the backlash of outraged loyalist opinion'.[30] On 11 October the first policeman to be killed by rioters, Constable Victor Arbuckle, was shot by a sniper while engaged with other R.U.C. men and soldiers in trying to hold back a hostile protestant crowd on the Shankill Road. But by the spring of 1970 the pattern was changing: the period of fraternisation between the catholics and the British army began to end when on 2 April rioting in the catholic area of Ballymurphy, in south-west Belfast, was put down by troops. Protestants claimed that the rioting was instigated by the I.R.A., the I.R.A. that it was due to Orange pro-

[29]See above, pp 38-9.
[30]Quoted in Boulton, *The U.V.F.*, p. 127.

vocation. From now onwards the I.R.A. increasingly appeared in action against the troops, while the fighting between the troops and the U.V.F. subsided. A familiar pattern was thus restored; and because the I.R.A. was now embroiled with the British army the 'protestant backlash' so often threatened and so long expected by newsmen, was delayed, though there were many thousands of licensed guns in protestant hands, and though these were being rapidly augmented illegally.

In August 1971 a new para-military organisation of working-class protestants, the Ulster Defence Association (U.D.A.), emerged to fight the I.R.A. in the general eruption of sectarian violence which followed the introduction of internment and which, in Belfast, caused the expulsion of thousands of working people, the great majority catholics, from their homes. U.D.A. men, in combat jackets and hoods, became a sinister feature of the worsening sectarian conflict. With the U.D.A. was closely associated Mr Billy Hull's Loyalist Association of Workers, based on several of the largest industrial plants in Belfast. Mr Hull announced at a great loyalist rally on 6 September 1971 in the Victoria Park, Belfast, that 'the age of the rubber bullet is over. It's lead bullets from now on. . . . We are British to the core but we won't hesitate to take on even the British if they attempt to sell our country down the river.'[31] From early in 1972 a new dimension was added to the violence by a succession of apparently random and motiveless murders, often preceded by torture, of civilians.[32] Of nearly 200 individual assassinations, the great majority have been of catholics, representing the 'protestant backlash' in its most gruesome and ferocious form; the remainder are assassinations, some committed before 1972, of protestant civilians by the I.R.A., though the I.R.A. do not regard themselves as being at war with protestants as such. Assassinations multiplied and the conflict grew more confused after the introduction of direct rule. The U.D.A. was torn by struggles over questions of leadership, strategy and ideology, and over the Mafia-like protection-rackets in which some U.D.A. leaders were notoriously involved. Controversy between the U.D.A. and Vanguard high-lights the conflict between working-class and middle-class interests among militant loyalists.

[31] Quoted in Boulton, *The U.V.F.*, p. 141.
[32] A study of these murders has just appeared: Martin Dillon and Denis Lehane, *Political murder in Northern Ireland* (London, 1973).

At the same time the U.D.A. were scarcely less hostile to the British army than to the I.R.A.; in September and October 1972 there was bitter fighting in Belfast between the U.D.A. and the troops, ending in a truce that was quickly followed by U.D.A. raids across the border in pursuance of an announced policy of carrying the war into the Republic. New protestant para-military formations emerged in 1973, of which the Ulster Freedom Fighters, apparently a break-away group of extreme elements in the U.V.F. and the U.D.A., announced in June that they had been responsible for assassinations of catholics during or since the previous summer. It was the first admission of its kind.

In its various manifestations and on its various levels the protestant violence of 1972-3, like the violence of the I.R.A., was to some extent motivated by sick minds and corrupt interests. But in general it would seem fundamentally to be the reaction of ordinary people, in an excess of fear, anger, despair, and passion for revenge, to the merciless and unending campaign of the Provos. Whereas the Provos claimed that their bombings and killings of policemen and soldiers and the destruction of shops, public houses (though in Belfast these were mostly owned by catholics) and factories, were directed against British imperialism, not against their protestant countrymen, protestants saw it all as directed against themselves and the Northern Ireland they were determined to maintain. The more militant of them reached the stage by the end of 1971 in which they identified the whole catholic community with the I.R.A., and set about retaliation by counter-terrorism aimed at catholics as such. And many peaceable and moderate protestants sorrowfully believe that the killing of innocent catholics will go on for as long as the Provos continue their attempt 'to bomb a million protestants into a catholic republic of all-Ireland'.

## 5 Nationalist reunion: the Social Democratic and Labour Party

While the unionist and extreme nationalist ranks have been splitting, the opposite process has been at work among moderate nationalists. A continuing cause of the ineffectiveness of the opposition at Stormont was not only its smallness in number but its internal divisions. In August 1970 six opposition members of the Stormont parliament, representing four separate groups, agreed to form the Social Democratic and Labour Party under the leadership of Mr Gerry Fitt, a labour M.P. both at Stormont and Westminster. Mr Fitt was a seasoned politician who had fought many elections in the republican socialist interest and lost very few. Coming 'straight out of the heart of Belfast's working class'[33], he had spent twelve years (1941-53) at sea when he began a life of intense political activity in his native town. He won a seat on the Belfast city council in 1958, became a member of the Stormont parliament for the Dock division of Belfast in 1962, and was returned to Westminster as member for West Belfast in 1966. He was a member of both parliaments when he became leader of the S.D.L.P. Tough and ebullient but mild and warm-hearted, he combines a fighting spirit with fervent devotion to peace, and socialist principles with a strong aspiration to Irish unity. His nationalism is forward-looking and free from bigotry. The other five founders of the S.D.L.P. were Messrs Ivan Cooper, Austin Currie, Paddy Devlin, John Hume and Paddy O'Hanlon, Messrs Cooper and Hume being leaders of the Derry Citizens' Action Committee. All firmly repudiated violence. All six except Mr Cooper were catholics, but all were vehement in insisting that the new party was non-sectarian. In contrast with old-style nationalism, the S.D.L.P. was committed to socialist principles, as well as to the eventual reunification of Ireland through the consent of the majority of people both in the north and in the south. The S.D.L.P. was far from including all opposition elements, but it was a large step towards that aim. Its six parliamentary spokesmen were unsparing in their efforts to obtain equality of citizenship and power-sharing for catholics, but continued frustration weakened their position as competitors with the I.R.A. for the allegiance of the catholic body. This in turn made it the more necessary for them to take a hard line against the internment of I.R.A. suspects, the ill-treatment of prisoners under interrogation, and brutalities committed by British soldiers. Over the refusal of government to institute an independent inquiry into the killing by soldiers of two civilians in Derry, they withdrew in a body from the Stormont parliament (15 July 1971) and refused to return, thereafter making internment the principal ground of their abstention, and setting up an 'alternative assembly'

[33]Michael McInerney in *Irish Times,* 20 Oct. 1973, p. 11.

—'the assembly of the Northern Irish people'—under the chairmanship of Mr Hume. From this political impasse they have apparently been extricated by the imposition of direct rule and the initiatives of Mr Whitelaw. For, despite internment, which still remains, though modified by Mr Whitelaw, they have cautiously decided to give his new assembly a trial; and, as we have seen, in the general election of June they have been returned with a marked, and perhaps decisive, increase in their parliamentary strength.

The S.D.L.P. are the new-style spokesmen of moderate catholic opinion. Believers in the power of reason, haters of violence and the sectarian mentality, and strenuous champions of social justice, they stand between two groups of violent extremists, catholics on the one hand, protestants on the other; and herein lies both a serious danger to their position and also a great political potentiality. They have shown exemplary tenacity, integrity and courage; and it is typical of the strain under which they live that the home of Mr Austin Currie near Dungannon has repeatedly been attacked by gunfire, and that on 17 December 1972 Mr Currie's wife, while he was absent, was brutally assaulted by armed intruders who scratched the letters U.V.F. on her chest. As a significant element in the new assembly the S.D.L.P. are specially concerned to secure an impartial police force on a community basis, which the police reforms since 1969 have not achieved, and a council of Ireland to facilitate cooperation with the Republic and prepare the way for eventual unity by agreement. They have been accepted by the government of the Republic, under both Mr Lynch and Mr Cosgrave, as the authentic voice of moderate nationalism in Northern Ireland, and the frequent conferences of their leaders with the taoiseach and his colleagues in Dublin are indicative of the community of interests and outlook that exists between the S.D.L.P. and the great majority of people in the Republic.

6  *The rise of a centre party*

The failure of parliamentary democracy in Northern Ireland had been reflected in the absence of any significant centre party to bridge the traditional protestant-catholic cleavage. In the crisis of January 1969 a com-

77

bination of liberal protestants and catholics was formed to support Captain O'Neill's reform-policy and to influence public opinion in favour of a new-style Northern Ireland. Its aims were

to heal our historic divisions and especially to effect recon-ciliaton between protestants and catholics, so that we may build a united community; to promote social justice and integrity in the political life of Ulster; to work for community peace through the democratic processes.[34]

This New Ulster Movement, whose chairman is Mr Brian Walker, has done valuable work in informing the public about current issues and stimulating political thinking on realistic lines, especially through its publication of lucid, reliable, and persuasive pamphlets, beginning with *The reform of Stormont* (June 1971), which advocated proportional representation and a system of practical power-sharing. The British government's constitutional proposals of March 1973 have much in common with N.U.M. ideas, especially as expressed in its seventh pam-phlet, *A new constitution for Northern Ireland* (August 1972).

The N.U.M. sought to exercise political influence but not to win political power. To win political power is the aim of the Alliance Party, founded in April 1970 and now under the chairmanship of Mr Oliver Napier. The party is pledged to work for 'complete and equal partnership in government and public life between protestants and catholics' while maintaining the union with Great Britain. It established branches in most constituencies and aspired to electoral successes in many of them. Two unionist members of the old Stormont parliament, Mr Thomas Gormley and Mr Phelim O'Neill, and one independent, Mr Robert McConnell, joined the new party. It was sadly disappointed when, in the elections for the new assembly, it won only eight of the 78 seats. But these eight have a strategic position in the assembly since they ensure a majority for the pro-assembly over the anti-assembly elements among the unionists.

[34]*Ireland—towards the return of the rule of law* (New Ulster Movement publication 8, Dec. 1972), p. [2]. For a complete list of N.U.M. publications, see bibliography, below, p. 120.

One of the paradoxes of the past five distracted years in
Northern Ireland is that bridgebuilding between the
divided communities has been making unprecedented progress. At the same time that O'Neill and Lemass were
encouraging good-neighbourliness between north and
south, the ecumenical movement was making a gradual but
significant impact in both parts of Ireland, and this helped
the bridgebuilding process. Long-standing organisations
dedicated to reconciliation, such as the Irish Association
for Cultural, Economic and Social Relations (founded in
1938), the Irish Christian Fellowship, and the Fellowship
of Reconciliation were reinvigorated. The Catholic
Social Study Conference widened its choice of speakers
invited to its annual sessions to include protestants, and
addressed itself especially to the problem of community
division. Many new organisations to promote peace and
social justice in Northern Ireland sprang up, such as the
Corrymeela Community, Protestant and Catholic En-
counter (P.A.C.E.), the New Ulster Movement, Women
Together, the Churches' Committee on Society, Redevelop-
ment and Peace (Sodepax), and Citizens United for
Reconciliation and Equality (C.U.R.E.). Never before have
such missionary efforts been made to heal community
division in Northern Ireland. And never before have the
churches, both severally and together, shown so much
concern to promote understanding and to condemn
violence.

Ecclesiastical organisation in Ireland is independent of
the political division of the country, and all the principal
churches of Northern Ireland extend across the border
Though the great majority of Irish catholics are in the
Republic, the primatial see of their church, as of the
Church of Ireland, is in Northern Ireland, at St Patrick's
city of Armagh.[35] While in Ireland as a whole the catholic
church has a large numerical preponderance (about 75%),
in Northern Ireland its members are outnumbered by
those of the protestant churches which, taken together,
account for 66% of the population. But if the churches in
Northern Ireland are taken singly, the catholic church is
the largest, and all are minority churches: in a population
of 1,500,000, about 500,000 belong to the catholic church,

[35]See above, pp 1-2.

nearly 400,000 to the presbyterian church, about 340,000 to the Church of Ireland, and about 70,000 to the methodist church. The presbyterian church (which has no connection with Rev. Mr Paisley's 'Free Presbyterian Church') is not only the largest of the protestant denominations but is historically the most distinctive element in Ulster protestantism. With only 5% of its total membership in the Republic it is more fully identified with Northern Ireland than any of the other principal churches, and it is no historical accident that its headquarters are in Belfast, while those of the Church of Ireland (and of the catholic church) are in Dublin. For these reasons, and because protestants are the dominant element in Northern Ireland, the attitudes of the presbyterian church towards the problems of a divided society are of special importance.

In the presbyterian general assembly sustained efforts have been made to examine protestant-catholic relations in a realistic and understanding spirit. It was resolved in 1965

that the assembly urge upon our own people humbly and frankly to acknowledge and to ask forgiveness for any attitudes and actions towards our Roman Catholic fellow countrymen which have been unworthy of our calling as followers of Jesus Christ; and that the assembly call upon our people to resolve to deal with all conflicts of interests, loyalties or beliefs in the spirit of charity rather than of suspicion and intolerance and in accordance with truth as set forth in the scriptures.[36]

In 1967 the assembly commended for study to kirk sessions and study groups a searching report on religious discrimination in Ireland by a committee headed by Rev. G. B. G. McConnell, minister of Donore Presbyterian Church, Dublin[37]. Applying the teaching and example of Jesus about the relations of Jews and Samaritans to protestant-catholic relations in Ireland, the report declared that 'we must accept as friends and brothers all those whom we meet, irrespective of race or creed. To

[36]*Minutes of the proceedings of the general assembly of the Presbyterian Church in Ireland, 1965,* p. 26 (9 June).
[37]Ibid., 1967, p. 59 (9 June).

promote sectarian strife, or to deny anyone his just rights on racial or credal grounds, is unchristian.' This did not mean that religious discrimination could never be justified: for example, Christian churches generally held that it was necessary to require a doctrinal test for admission to the Christian ministry, and in making certain medical appointments religious discrimination might be defended because of differences between protestant and catholic ethics in the field of obstetrics. But unless religious principles thus had a direct bearing on the case, discrimination on the ground of religion could never be justified. The report recognised and deplored the reality of unjustifiable religious discrimination in many spheres of life, mainly in Northern Ireland but also to some extent in the Republic (as in the prohibition of the sale of contraceptives and the censorship of publications on family planning). It noted the possibility that much of this discrimination had its roots in religious segregation at the school level. It pointed out that there was a tendency to exclude catholics from social activities of the presbyterian church largely through fear of mixed marriages. 'We firmly believe that the enforcement of the *ne temere* decree is in large measure responsible for this. Many feel that the decree is a serious case of religious discrimination, and that the Roman Catholic church has no right to bind the consciences of non-Roman-Catholics.' The report concluded:

In view of our long history of racial, political and religious division . . . we realise that the elimination of religious discrimination is no easy task, but we welcome the signs that we are moving in the right direction. We believe that ventures of trust and cooperation will usually meet with a response and we pray that in all our relationships we may be led to speak and act in the spirit of that divine love which is at the heart of the gospel.[38]

The spirit expressed in these statements continued to be voiced by the presbyterian church after the outbreak of sectarian violence. During the civil rights disturbances of October 1968 the assembly's 'government committee' called on all church members 'to take to heart the shame and danger of our situation':

we are the more concerned, as Christians, because religious

[38]*General assembly of the presbyterian church in Ireland, 1967, annual reports,* pp 120-30.

loyalties have been used to foster social enmity and party interests, rather than inspiring concern for human need, for truth and justice, for self-denial and reconciliation.

After the fighting of January 1969 the committee declared:

In what has happened we are reaping the harvest of mutual suspicion and fear, of non-cooperation, vested interests and party advantage . . . . . . Those who hoped for an uneasy peace, by preserving the status quo or by a gradual improvement in relationships without seriously disturbing the established pattern, do not seem to have realised the passions which have been welling up in situations to which they had become uncritically accustomed. There has been, for too long, a conspiracy of silence . . . .

Although our general assembly and church have repeatedly spoken out on issues of social injustice and have tried to act in fairness to our fellow-citizens of whatever communion, we must confess that we have not done so with sufficient zeal and urgency, sufficient self-examination and self-denial . . .[39]

In October 1972 the 'general board' of the general assembly unreservedly condemned attacks on catholic church buildings, offered sympathy to all whose homes and businesses had suffered damage, and reaffirmed 'the strong obligation on ourselves and on all who seek for peace to respect the public forces of law and order, and to resist the gangster and terrorist, no matter what cause they profess. Those who advocate enmity or violence must share responsibility with those who practice it.' In November 1972 the assembly's 'government committee', commenting on Mr Whitelaw's green paper (*The future of Northern Ireland*), declared:

Christians have a calling to be peacemakers, not men of violence We are under obligation both to public justice and public order. We must be faithful to our beliefs, fearless in witnessing to what we judge as right and true, yet owing respect to those who carry public responsibilities for government and security

And in expectation of the British constitutional proposals the same committee wrote in February 1973:

Political aims and loyalties have their proper place, but as

[39]The Presbyterian Church in Ireland, *The Northern Ireland situation*, no. 1 (Belfast, 1972), p. 16.

servants not enemies of the common good. Partizan attitudes and demands will never bring that peace of mutual reconciliation and cooperation which our land needs. Habits of domination or of opposition are alike at fault. A change of heart is needed, not just from one section of the community or one part of Ireland but from all.[40]

Such declarations can be paralleled in the other protestant churches and in the catholic church;[41] and church leaders of all denominations have actively engaged in social and community efforts of many kinds directed towards constructive peace-making.

For the first time protestant and catholic clergy, instead of identifying themselves with the combatants, as in the past, have shown a remarkable degree of solidarity in standing out against violence, from whatever quarter it has come. The heads of the principal churches have repeatedly issued joint statements on the subject, of which that of 9 February 1973 made the point that 'the appalling horror of the past four years in Northern Ireland . . . . has shocked the whole world', but 'it has also shocked the overwhelming majority of people in Northern Ireland'.

Hundreds of thousands of deeply committed Christians here utterly reject the savage deeds of tiny bands of extremists. At the same time we must all examine our consciences humbly before God . . . Each one of us must do all in his power to purge from his own heart all feelings of bitterness or partizanship. Now is the time for us to take every opportunity of meeting together and seeking the common good . . . We have the example of many of the relatives of people who have died from violence here and who, even in their sorrow, spoke only words of forgiveness and peace. Persons in public life have a most grave responsibility . . . before God to work unceasingly for a just and lasting political settlement—even if it involves moving away from entrenched positions. The general public, too, of which we are all a part, has a grave responsibility, and must shake itself loose from over-rigid political attitudes.[42]

This was signed by the two archbishops of Armagh (Most Rev. Dr. William, Cardinal, Conway, and Most Rev.

[40]*The Northern Ireland situation*, no. 2 (1973), pp 5, 6.
[41]See, for example, *Violence in Ireland and Christian conscience, from addresses given by Cahal B. Daly, Bishop of Ardagh and Clonmacnoise* (Dublin, 1973).
[42]*The Northern Ireland situation*, no. 2, p. 10.

Dr G. O. Simms), by the moderator of the presbyterian general assembly (Rt Rev. Dr Victor Lynas), and by the president of the methodist church (Rev. E. R. Lindsay).

The significance of all this for reconciliation is qualified by the fact that, on the one hand, despite the affirmations of churches and church leaders, individual clergy continue to be in varying degrees involved in extremist politics, and, on the other, that respect for ecclesiastical authority has appreciably declined among the laity, both protestant and catholic. No one has more firmly and courageously condemned the violence of the I.R.A. than the catholic bishop of Down and Connor, Most Rev. Dr William Philbin, but he has been openly defied by catholics on the streets of Belfast; and the same is true of protestant clergy who have made a stand against protestant terrorists. Even among the large majority of laymen who do respect the clergy the tendency to polarisation becomes almost irresistible with the prolongation of the fighting. Yet the attitude of the churches towards the conflict, however limited its immediate effects may be, does at least mark a new beginning in community relations, and does prove that the conflict is not a religious war, even though the combatants have to be described by denominational labels. An unprecedented manifestation of the new spirit is the decision of the catholic bishops to convene on 26 September at Dundalk (in the Republic, but about halfway between Belfast and Dublin) a conference of representatives of all the main Christian churches, to survey the areas of agreement and of disagreement between them and to consider certain crucial problems such as mixed marriages. The initiative of the catholic bishops has met with a general and positive response, and the intended conference is to be presided over jointly by the catholic archbishop of Armagh, as chairman of the Irish Episcopal Conference, and by the protestant archbishop of Armagh, as chairman of the Irish Council of Churches. This Dundalk conference project is perhaps the most significant gesture against the sectarian spirit ever made in Ireland, and has important implications for Christianity in the world.

How much real progress towards reconciliation has been made at the grassroots is, of course, uncertain, but there are indications that profound changes in political and social thinking are taking place. These are a response not only to the force of peaceful persuasion but also to the brutal facts of the apparently endless sectarian fighting. In this connection the trade union movement has played a significant part both in transcending the sectarian divide in the north and in maintaining a measure of working-class solidarity as between north and south.

Sectarian conflict, which has accompanied the industrial growth of Belfast and the Lagan valley for more than a century, retarded, but did not prevent the development of labour organisation in the north, on the British model; nor did the political differences between Belfast and Dublin prevent their trades councils from combining (in 1894) to form an Irish Trade Union Congress. Within the Orange fold itself working-class influences in Belfast during the first decade of the present century sought to break with official unionist attitudes, and to democratise and nationalise the Orange tradition. The Independent Loyal Orange Institution was founded in 1903 as a working-class protest against the domination of the official Orange Order by employers and landlords; and under the inspiration of Robert Lindsay Crawford it gave voice to a new kind of nationalism:

We consider that it is high time that Irish protestants should consider their position as Irish citizens in their attitude towards their Roman Catholic countrymen, and that the latter should choose once and for all between nationality or sectarianism. In an Ireland in which protestant and catholic stand sullen and discontented, it is not too much to hope for that they will reconsider their positions and in their common trials unite on a basis of nationality . . . There is room in Ireland for a patriotic party with a sound constructive policy that will devote itself to the task of freeing the country from the domination of impracticable creeds and organised tyrannies and to securing the urgent and legitimate redress of her many grievances.[43]

Crawford's ascendancy in a new organisation proved short-lived: official unionist orthodoxy was soon reasserted and he was expelled in 1908 from the Independent Orange Order he had helped to found.[44] Working-class solidarity developed on a less dangerous and dramatic level.

[43]Manifesto issued from Magheramorne, Co. Antrim, 'from the Independent Orangemen of Ireland' to 'all Irishmen whose country stands first in their affections', 13 July 1905, quoted in J. W. Boyle, 'The Belfast Protestant Association and the Independent Orange Order, 1901-10' in *Irish Historical Studies,* xiii, no. 50 (Sept. 1962), p. 135.

[44]See John Boyle, as above, pp 117-52.

The Irish Trade Union Congress survived the partition of Ireland in 1920-22, and within it there emerged the antecedents of the labour parties in the two Irish parliaments. But the Irish Trade Union Congress became split in 1945 over the conflicting claims of British-based and Irish-based unions, the large majority of organised workers in the north belonging to the former, while in the south about half belonged to the latter. Over against the old T.U.C., to which the British-based and some of the Irish-based unions adhered, there arose a rival Congress of Irish Unions, and it seemed as if the split in the trade-union movement would eventually parallel the political division of Ireland. Instead, the idea of an all-Ireland movement prevailed, and unity was restored with the establishment of the Irish Congress of Trade Unions in 1959, at a time when the I.R.A. was waging a guerilla campaign against Northern Ireland. A Northern Ireland committee of the old T.U.C. had been formed in 1943 and this was maintained under the new congress, though the northern unions might well have converted it into a separate northern congress. The government of Northern Ireland refused recognition to the northern committee because it was part of a Dublin-based congress, but the northern trade unionists held their ground and eventually gained their point in 1964, when the pressure of mounting unemployment caused Captain O'Neill's government to yield. In 1966 the president of the I.C.T.U., Mr Fintan Kennedy, was able in an address to congress to say of Captain O'Neill: 'we see in him an expression of the same Christian idealism on which our own movement is based, and we say to him: "Neighbour, well done" '.[45] In December of that year the Northern Ireland Committee of the I.C.T.U. and the Northern Ireland Parliamentary Labour Party discussed with members of the northern cabinet such crucial demands as reform of the local government franchise, the removal of religious discrimination, the representation of minorities on government-appointed public bodies, and the creation of the office of ombudsman. When the present disturbances began, the northern leaders were enabled to exercise a moderating influence on the situation through their own

[45]Quoted in Charles McCarthy, 'Civil strife and the growth of trade union unity: the case of Ireland' in *Government and Opposition*, vii. no. 4 (Autumn 1973), p. 423, a pioneer study to which I am much indebted.

autonomous committee (of which the chairman was then Mr Stephen McGonagle, a Derry man and a catholic, who was made vice-chairman of the new Derry Development Commission in 1969), and through their affiliation with the I.C.T.U. on the one hand and with the British labour and trade union movement on the other. They strongly backed Captain O'Neill's reforming efforts, and in the general election that he called in 1969 they urged all trade unionists to support only candidates

who are known to be genuinely non-sectarian; who have un-equivocally declared themselves for equal citizenship and equal opportunities for all, and who have shown themselves to be sympathetic to the aims of the trade-union movement.[46]

It is all too obvious that such sentiments did not prevent protestant and catholic working-men from engaging in ruinous conflict with one another, as they had done so often in the past. But what is not so well recognised is that trade-union influence has done much to prevent the extension of sectarian violence from the ghettos to the shop floor. The most dramatic instance occurred in the Belfast shipyard of Harland and Wolff on 15 August 1969, after a night of the worst rioting of that year in the city. Great tension had built up among the 8,000 workers in the yard, and there was imminent danger of an explosion of violence, such as had occurred in the early 20s, against the small minority of catholic workers, which would be the signal for a general outbreak of sectarian bloodshed in Belfast's workshops, factories and docks. All this was averted by the initiative of two leading shop-stewards, Mr Sandy Scott and Mr James McFall, both protestants and both men of vision, moral courage, and great commonsense. In consultation with the other shop-stewards of the yard, they organised a monster meeting of shipyard workers and persuaded them to make a com-mitment 'to maintain peace and goodwill in the shipyard and throughout the province'. The platform party included the acting lord-mayor of Belfast; Mr Roy Bradford, then minister of commerce; and Rev. Eric Gallagher, a well-known methodist minister. Mr Scott presided and was phenomenally successful in keeping control of his vast audience. He argued that if violence spread to the yard, its whole work-programme would be endangered, orders

[46]Ibid., p. 425.

would be cancelled, and massive unemployment would result; and he appealed to their consciences and their sense of human dignity. Mr Gallagher stressed the latter point and led the meeting in a communal prayer for peace and brotherhood.[47] That night Mr Scott and Mr McFall visited the Falls Road and other catholic areas to persuade catholic workers who had stayed away from the shipyard that they could safely return to work next day. At the barricades the password that gained them immediate admission was 'Scott and McFall, yard shop-stewards'. They and other shop-stewards also helped to form 'do-it-yourself peace-keeping organisations' in the combustible working-class and mainly protestant area of East Belfast, where a sustained and combined effort of laymen and clergy succeeded in keeping the peace. Among these was Mr David Bleakley, then chairman of the East Belfast Peace Committee.[48]

The position thus gained has been more or less held; when Mr Paisley on 30 September 1969 called for 100,000 workers to down tools and join him in a parade to Stormont to protest against 'appeasement' by the government, the response of the shipyard workers was derisory. The Northern Ireland Committee of the I.C.T.U. has steadily backed the government's reform-programme and steadily exerted pressure for industrial development, full employment, and adequate housing. On the suspension of the Stormont parliament it called on trade-unionists to support the new administration of Mr Whitelaw, and appealed to those who had withdrawn their services from public bodies to return. As the killings multiplied, shop-stewards took the lead in linking the 'right to work' with the 'right to live', and were backed by the Northern Ireland Committee. It remains true that northern workers tend to keep their identity as trade-unionists separate from their political identity; thus, although there are some 215,000 trade unionists in Northern Ireland, the Northern Ireland Labour Party has succeeded in returning only one member to the new assembly, Mr David Bleakley. Mr Sandy Scott himself received only 854 first-preference

---

[47]Michael McInerney, *Trade union bid for peace in the north* (Irish Times, 1970), pp 8-12. This perceptive piece of contemporary reporting and interpretation is reprinted from the *Irish Times*, Dec. 1969-Jan. 1970.

[48]See his book, *Peace in Ulster* (London, 1972), pp 71-3, 89-98; and see above, pp 41, 55-6.

votes in a poll of 75,000 in South Antrim, and was eliminated on the sixth count.

## 8 The northern troubles and the Irish Republic

Friendly relations between the two Irish governments had continued after the retirement of Lemass in November 1966. The new taoiseach, Mr Jack Lynch, visited Captain O'Neill at Stormont (December 1966) and received him at Merrion Street (January 1967). On Captain O'Neill's fifth anniversary as prime minister the *Irish Press* praised him for the progress he had made against formidable obstacles in promoting harmony between protestants and catholics in the north, and suggested that the O'Neill-Lemass meetings would become an accepted part of the pattern of Irish politics (March 1968). The outbreak of violence in the north in the autumn of 1968 and the resignation of Captain O'Neill in April 1969 upset all this. North-south relations quickly deteriorated. As violence in the north mounted and spread, most northern protestants came to see the Dublin government only as hostile and hypocritical—conniving at, if not secretly approving, the blatant use of its territory as a training-ground and a refuge by the I.R.A. in their offensive against the northern government. The notorious fact that the chief of staff of the Provos, Seán Mac Stiofáin (formerly John Stephenson), lived openly (till May 1972) in the Republic, and that I.R.A. communiqués, claiming or disclaiming responsibility for the latest bombings and killings in the north, issued in a steady stream from headquarters in Dublin seemed to prove the hollowness of Mr Lynch's repeated condemnation of violence. Yet viewed in historical perspective, there was nothing surprising in all this.

The I.R.A. is essentially an all-Ireland organisation and the I.R.A. tradition has long roots. It was difficult for citizens of the Republic not to feel some sympathy with the 'freedom-fighters' in the north, however much they might detest their methods. It was difficult for Mr Lynch to bring the law effectively to bear on I.R.A. activities, especially because, though the I.R.A. itself was illegal, it had a legal 'front' in Sinn Féin, which was a registered political party. Moreover the struggle in the north was brought home to Irishmen throughout the Republic with unprecedented actuality, and almost blow by blow, by the national television service, Radio Telefís Eireann.

When the catholics of the Bogside were being savaged by the R.U.C. (April 1969), when over 500 catholic homes were burnt by protestants in Belfast in a few days (August 1969), when British troops descended on the Lower Falls in search of arms (July 1970), when hundreds of catholics were interned at one stroke (9 August 1971), and, above all, when thirteen unarmed catholic youths were killed by paratroopers in Derry on 'bloody Sunday' (30 January 1972), one of the strongest collective emotions in the Republic was roused, and pressure on the Dublin government to intervene forcibly was at times very severe. The marvel is that intervention went no further than private and secret support for the I.R.A., the diversion to the Provos of public money voted for relief of distress, and an abortive scheme to facilitate the illegal importation of arms through Dublin airport. Despite their conviction that the northern problem was rooted in partition and could in the long run only be remedied by reunification, the great majority in the Republic increasingly disapproved of the I.R.A. campaign and had no wish to see hostilities extended to the south. Mr Lynch correctly interpreted these attitudes by his constant repudiation of violence and his efforts to promote a peaceful settlement, while at the same time firmly rejecting the claim of northern unionists that the affairs of Northern Ireland were none of his business.

Mr Lynch's northern policy brought him at once into collision with three of his most senior ministers—Mr Charles Haughey (minister for finance), Mr Neil Blaney (minister for agriculture), and Mr Kevin Boland (minister for local government)—who formed a group within the cabinet that ardently wanted the Republic to intervene in support of the hard-pressed northern catholics. Mr Lynch, holding office by a very narrow majority, was put in a position of excruciating difficulty and complexity from which he eventually extricated himself by dismissing Mr Haughey and Mr Blaney (May 1970) and prosecuting them and others on a charge of conspiracy to import arms illegally (September-October). Mr Boland resigned in protest at the dismissals, and, though the prosecution of Mr Haughey and Mr Blaney failed, the political victory lay with Mr Lynch. He averted a threatened split in his party (Fianna Fáil) and twice obtained a resounding expression of popular support which, though the north was not the issue on either occasion, was generally felt to be an endorsement of his northern policy. On both occasions the issue was a constitutional referendum, the first (10 May 1972) on the proposed entry of the Republic into the E.E.C., the second (7 December 1972) on the proposed removal of the clause in the constitution in which the state recognised 'the special position of the Holy Catholic Apostolic and Roman Church as the guardian of the faith professed by the great majority of the citizens' (article 44, §2). The decision on the E.E.C., by a majority of 83%, was a dramatic departure from the traditional republican attitude towards national sovereignty, and all the more telling because Sinn Féin had campaigned strenuously against it. So indeed had the labour party, but on economic and social grounds that made its case quite distinct from that of Sinn Féin. Unionist opinion in Northern Ireland was generally favourable to the E.E.C. decision, which meant that both parts of Ireland became part of the E.E.C. on 1 January 1973. On the second referendum the poll was only 51% but the majority in favour was 84%. Neither in the Republic nor in Northern Ireland was this change in the constitution seen as an important step to that 'new kind of Irish society, equally agreeable to north and south' which Mr Lynch had said (23 February 1971) he wanted to bring about. Yet as the first amendment to the constitution made as a friendly gesture to protestants throughout Ireland the change was of great historical significance.

When internment was introduced by Mr Faulkner there were angry exchanges between him and Mr Lynch, who declared his support for the civil disobedience campaign and called for an end of the Stormont regime: 'as an immediate objective of political action the Stormont government should be replaced by an administration in which power and decision-making will be equally shared by unionist and non-unionist' (12 August 1971). A week later Mr Lynch sent a telegram to Mr Heath and Mr Faulkner then meeting at Chequers, condemning internment and the current military operations in the north: 'solutions require to be found through political means and should be based on the principle of immediate and full equality of treatment for everyone in Northern Ireland' (19 August). Mr Heath described this statement as 'unjustifiable in its contents [and] unacceptable in its attempt to interfere in the affairs of the United Kingdom'. Nevertheless a meeting which had previously been arranged between him and Mr Lynch took place at Chequers on 6-7 September, and a second meeting, at which Mr Faulkner was also present, on 27-8 September. An agreed statement issued after the second Chequers meeting declared: 'we are at one in condemning any form of violence as an instrument of political pressure, and it is our common purpose to seek to bring violence and internment and all other emergency measures to an end without delay'. Thus in effect the Republic's claim to be vitally interested in any northern settlement was recognised. Mr Lynch's position was strengthened by the fall of the Stormont regime and the introduction of direct rule under Mr Whitelaw. The northern conflict became a matter of friendly consultation between the Irish and the British governments and spokesmen of the principal non-violent groups in the north. At the same time Mr Lynch took a tougher line with the I.R.A. in the Republic, setting up a special criminal court (26 May 1972), arresting Seán Mac Stiofáin (19 November), and amending the Offences against the State Act to facilitate the prosecution of members of illegal organisations (3 December).

Mr Whitelaw's green paper (October 1972), in a notable section on 'The Irish dimension', affirmed that 'no United Kingdom government for many years has had any wish to impede the realisation of Irish unity, if it were to come about by genuine and freely given mutual agreement', and went on:

Whatever arrangements are made for the future administration of Northern Ireland [they] must take account of the province's relationship with the Republic of Ireland; and to the extent that this is done, there is an obligation upon the Republic to reciprocate. Both the economy and the security of the two areas are to some considerable extent interdependent, and the same is true of both in their relationship with Great Britain. It is therefore clearly desirable that any new arrangements for Northern Ireland should, whilst meeting the wishes of Northern Ireland and Great Britain, be as far as possible acceptable to and accepted by the Republic of Ireland, which from 1 January 1973 will share the rights and obligations of membership of the European community.[49]

This, however non-committal, marked a large advance in British understanding of the Northern Ireland question. But the green paper also sought to reassure unionists by its promise of a 'border poll', and accordingly the first

[49]*The future of Northern Ireland: a paper for discussion* (London, 1972), pp 33-4.

of an intended series of plebiscites was held on 8 March. To the question 'do you want Northern Ireland to remain part of the United Kingdom?' 591,820 electors answered 'yes', and 6,463 to the question 'do you want Northern Ireland to be joined with the Republic outside the United Kingdom?' The voting on the first question was entirely predictable and was regarded by unionists as a conclusive decision against any reopening of the question for ten years, when another plebiscite would be held. The smallness of the vote on the second question was the direct result of widespread boycotting of the poll by nationalists, a policy which was extensively approved in the Republic.

The defeat of Mr Lynch's government in the general election of 28 February 1973 by a national coalition, led by Mr Liam Cosgrave, of the two opposition parties, Fine Gael and the labour party, was not a defeat for Mr Lynch's policy on Northern Ireland. References to Northern Ireland in the election campaign were generally muted, but while Sinn Fein was unable to return a single one of its candidates, both elements of the coalition were known to be strongly committed to working for a peaceful solution and enforcing the law against the I.R.A. In Dr Conor Cruise O'Brien, one of the labour party chiefs, whom the general election brought to office as minister for posts and telegraphs, the new government included an advocate for realism and humanity on the Northern Ireland question whose insight, courage and energy were equalled by his world-wide reputation as a writer. As in Britain the change from labour to a conservative government in 1970 brought no permanent change in policy towards Northern Ireland, so in the Republic the replacement of Fianna Fail by the national coalition has not fundamentally altered, though it has appreciably improved, relations with Northern Ireland and with Britain. Mr Cosgrave's government like that of his predecessor, declares that the ultimate solution of the Northern Ireland problem lies in the reunification of Ireland not by the coercion of the unionists but by their voluntary partnership in a single state. It recognises that this consummation may lie indefinitely in the future, and seeks in the meanwhile, by a policy of friendly relations both with the people of Northern Ireland and with the British government, to assist in bringing about an end to the violence, reconciliation between the divided communities in the north, and practical cooperation between Northern Ireland and the Republic.

## IX

## ULSTER AND IRELAND

Ulster has always had its own geographical and historical identity, but it is also part of Ireland, historically as well as geographically. Its problems can only be understood in the context of Irish history; and the same is true of the diminished Ulster that emerged as the separate political entity of Northern Ireland in 1920.

The passions and the violence that have ravaged Northern Ireland since 1968 have been due in part to problems characteristic of contemporary industrial society elsewhere—chronic unemployment, inadequate and insufficient housing, a heightened sense of deprivation and frustration in face of expanding education and rising material standards. There is nothing peculiar to Northern Ireland in civil rights marches and sit-downs or in violence as a form of group protest. And there are ample precedents outside Ireland for such phenomena as the 'tartan gangs' and the 'protection' rackets that flourish in the pathological conditions of life in parts of Belfast. Economic pressures aggravate the disorder and the suffering, but the roots of the present troubles lie in centuries of political and cultural division within Ulster whose disastrous legacy to Northern Ireland has been a tradition of ascendancy, discrimination, sectarianism, and disaffection. This does not mean that economic and social factors do not enter deeply into the problem: in the seventeenth century protestants were the dispossessors, catholics the dispossessed, and it remains true that, as between protestants and catholics, the distribution of wealth is much more favourable to the former than the latter.

One way in which the present phase of the Ulster question is unique is that, for the first time, the daily course of events in Ulster has been reflected in the television screen as well as in the public press. Television has exceptional capacity for high-lighting what is most sensational in the immediate situation; and violence in Northern Ireland since October 1968 has been continuously, and sometimes consciously, enacted before television cameras. The effects of this on the viewing public (including actual participants in the violence) have not been assessed and may not be assessable. But it can scarcely be doubted that the vicarious experience of violence has some influence on public opinion, whether by way of revulsion, or of attraction, or, more likely, of callousness induced by familiarity. Viewers in Northern Ireland can all receive the programmes of the B.B.C. and of U.T.V. (the independent television system in Northern Ireland), but only a small minority those of Radio Telefís Eireann, whereas in the Republic, while all viewers can receive R.T.E. programmes, a high proportion of those in the most populous eastern region also receive the British programmes. News of the same controversial events inevitably assumes a different complexion in the hands of an Irish and of a British television service, but while large numbers of viewers in the Republic can compare Irish and British coverage of the same events, comparatively few in Northern Ireland can do so (though they can, of course compare B.B.C. coverage with that of U.T.V.). The loss to Northern Ireland viewers is, perhaps, most regrettable in the field of news commentaries and public affairs discussion, where a high level of honesty, insight and realism has often been attained, for example in the distinguished commentaries of Mr Liam Hourican as R.T.E. correspondent in Belfast. In seeking to present the thinking and the outlook of advocates of violence as an aspect of the conflict in Northern Ireland R.T.E. journalists ran into serious difficulties with the government of Mr Lynch, which alleged that the national broadcasting service was being used to the detriment of government policy. The R.T.E. Authority, for its part, held that it was endeavouring to fulfil its statutory duty of maintaining impartiality and objectivity in its treatment of controversial issues. Relations became so strained that the government eventually used its statutory powers to dismiss the entire R.T.E. Authority (24 November 1972). One result of all this is that I.R.A. spokesmen have received far more exposure on British than on Irish television.

The troubles in Northern Ireland have attracted unprecedented attention from voluntary organisations, religious, philanthropic, and scientific, both within Ireland and from outside. All these are attempting, with varying resources and expertness, to alleviate suffering, to promote communication between the conflicting forces, to investigate the causes of conflict, and to explore possibilities of settlement. Many groups and individuals are thus involved, and a great deal of activity is going on, mostly behind the scenes. Some of it is having positive and immediate results, some of it promises to add greatly to our knowledge and understanding of the Ulster problem as it is today.

Seen in the perspective of history, the problem has its roots in the early seventeenth century when Ulster, for many centuries the stronghold of Gaelic power and Gaelic culture, became the setting of a British and protestant colony designed to establish British power and British culture once and for all on the ruins of a defeated Gaelic and catholic world. The colony proved more successful than any other British colony in Ireland before or since—proved in the long run too successful, since it created that divided society which is the core of the present northern problem. The protestant community in Ulster served British interests as well as its own by its conscious separation from, and sense of superiority to, the expropriated catholic community. Whenever British power in Ireland since the early-seventeenth century was seriously threatened—in 1641-9, 1688-91, 1794-8, 1886, 1893, and 1916-21—protestant Ulster was vitally involved, and on each occasion was an important, and sometimes a decisive, factor in the resistance to Irish attempts to win self-government. Twice—in 1641-9 and 1688-91—the resistance of protestant Ulster helped to decide the outcome of a revolutionary situation in Britain. In 1689 the successful defence of Derry by its citizens against its Jacobite besiegers, followed by the victory of the Enniskilleners at Newtownbutler over their Jacobite assailants, proved disastrous to the catholic cause in Ulster, and prepared the way for the decisive confrontation in 1690 at the River Boyne between the two kings whose rivalry for the throne of England was identified with the conflict between catholics and protestants in Ireland. The defeat of the deposed king, the catholic James II, by his protestant supplanter, King William III, was a major event not only in Irish and British history but also in the history of Europe; for William III, prince of Orange and ruler of the Netherlands, was the head of a European coalition to resist the aggressions of Louis XIV of France, who was James II's patron and backer, For protestants, and especially Ulster protestants, the anniversary of the battle of the Boyne[1] became an occasion for ritual rejoicing over their deliverance from a triple danger.

Though loyalty to the British crown has been a dominant characteristic of protestant Ulster, there have been signs during the past 350 years that this loyalty is not unconditional: in 1639, in the last quarter of the eighteenth century, in 1912-14, and since direct rule was introduced in 1972, resentment against British policy has brought protestant elements in Ulster to a state of disaffection and, in 1798, even to rebellion. But only in 1912-14 was there anything approaching solidarity in protestant defiance of British authority, and then the would-be rebels were acting in collaboration with British tories. Though Ulster protestantism had never had a monolithic character before the crisis that led to the creation of Northern Ireland, at only one of the earlier political crises of their history did Ulster protestants join in significant numbers with catholics in opposition to Britain—in the era of the European 'enlightenment', when Ulster radicals were in the forefront of a movement that linked the cause of liberal and democratic reform with that of national unity and independence. Their involvement in the United Irishmen proved to be an aberration for Ulster protestants, and the enthusiasm so many of them had shown for the rights of catholics and a democratic Ireland became submerged in a general conversion to Orangeism and the necessity of defending protestant ascendancy and the union with Great Britain against catholic and nationalist pressure. From the early-nineteenth century onwards the whole course of Ulster politics has been dominated by the determination of Ulster protestants to remain within an overwhelmingly protestant state, the United Kingdom, and not to become part of a self-governing Ireland which, in an age of growing democracy, would be subject to a preponderantly catholic parliament and government. The radicalism inherent in the Ulster protestant character has thus been stunted by being forced into an iron mould of political conformity; and working-class interests and action in an industrialised society, deflected from the pattern normal to Britain and industrial countries on the Continent, have been sacrificed to endemic sectarian conflict.

In frustrating the efforts of nationalists to include them

[1] 1 July according to old-style dating, 12 July from 1752, when the British calendar was brought into line with the new-style dating on the Continent.

97

in a self-governing Ireland, Ulster unionists were taking up the same position in relation to Ireland as that of nationalists in relation to the United Kingdom; and just as the nationalist secession from the United Kingdom would have placed northern unionists in a permanent minority in an unpartitioned Ireland, so the secession of the six counties from Ireland placed catholics in a permanent minority in that area. The experience of fifty years of home rule has fostered some of the attributes of nationality among protestants in Northern Ireland; and a U.D.I. outlook has been strengthened by the sense of being abandoned by Britain now felt by some of those protestants who see that the age of protestant ascendancy in a Northern Ireland within the United Kingdom is over. The idea of national self-determination for Northern Ireland remains vague, and those who appear to be its strongest champions, such as Mr Craig and perhaps Mr Taylor, take care not to define it. If it means protestant ascendancy in an independent six counties it offers no prospect of a settlement, since catholics would not accept it; if it implies political partnership between the two communities it at least holds out a theoretical possibility. But the only likelihood of such a partnership emerging seems to lie in the context of the new assembly that the British government has designed for Northern Ireland and that Mr Craig and his supporters seem bent on wrecking. The precedent of 'colonial nationalism' in Ireland of the late eighteenth century is not encouraging; and the short-lived support given to the home-rule movement in its origins a century ago by protestants smarting with resentment against Gladstone for disestablishing the protestant episcopal church suggests that unionist hostility to reforms imposed from London is a very weak basis for unionist collaboration with nationalism. In any case the concept of a separate nation in the north-east, and therefore of two Irish nations in Ireland, is passionately rejected, on the one hand by the great majority of protestants in Northern Ireland, to whom the thought of abandoning their British nationality and forfeiting British subsidies is abhorrent, and on the other hand by Irish nationalists in Northern Ireland and in the Republic alike, however moderate or however extreme their nationalism. If the protestant idea of U.D.I. were to be extended to all nine of the Ulster counties instead of applying only to the six, it would have something in common with the Provos' idea of an Ulster provincial parliament and government. But there is nothing to suggest that Mr Craig would favour any arrangement whereby a protestant majority of two-thirds in six counties would be exchanged for a bare, if any, protestant majority in nine counties; still less would the position of a province in the federated Irish republic of the Provos' scheme be likely to attract Ulster protestants in significant numbers. The two-nation idea seems to make historical sense only as a way of recognising that the conflict in Northern Ireland is basically between the majority who wish to remain part of a British nation and a minority who seek reunion with an Irish nation.

In a coexistence of over 350 years the two communities in Ulster have, of course, interacted strongly on each other. Protestant Ulster is not just an outlying part of British society, nor is catholic Ulster indistinguishable from the rest of catholic Ireland. Some of the characteristics of a shared-culture have long existed in Ulster speech (though it is English), in Ulster humour, in Ulster folk-songs and folk-ways, and in a certain stern and realistic attitude to life exemplified by a preoccupation with religion for its own sake. The common interests of small farmers in the country-side have cut across the sectarian divide. The rise of an Ulster theatre tradition and of an Ulster group of poets, novelists and painters has given expression to the sense of an Ulster community; and the vigorous and many-sided growth since 1908 of the Queen's University of Belfast, always a meeting-place of protestants and catholics, has been in part a cause and in part a result of this sense of community transcending religious division. While partition has in some ways accentuated the cleavage between pro-testants and catholics, in other ways it has tended to bring the two elements together as common beneficiaries of a local administration more responsive to local needs and local problems—as in education and the social services— than the pre-1920 British administration of Ireland ever was. All these things are indications of a regional identity shared by protestants and catholics, but they do not amount to evidence of a national community, which usually implies a population united by pride in a common past and by the will to share a common future.

The attempt now being made to restore autonomy in Northern Ireland on a basis of equality of citizenship and a sharing of power between majority and minority requires a measure of mutual confidence between the divided communities and mutual respect for two distinct national ideals, hitherto incompatible. Mutual confidence and respect are not plants that flourish in conditions of chronic violence, but revulsion against the methods both of the I.R.A. and of protestant extremists has induced a good deal of new thinking in the great mass of people, protestant and catholic, who are of neither extreme. The idea of a new deal for all Ireland, involving the rejection of existing political dogmas and the values of the affluent society, is making some progress among protestants and catholics on both sides of the border. An example is the New Ireland Movement, whose most dedicated and persuasive spokesman is Mr John D. A. Robb[2] a young Ulster presbyterian, who, as surgeon at the Royal Victoria Hospital, Belfast, had been in daily contact with the consequences of communal violence. This New Ireland Movement might be regarded as an updated version of the United Irish movement in its constitutional and idealist phase.

The United Irishmen failed partly because they combined a civil rights movement with a separatist movement, and therefore challenged simultaneously the privileged position of the ruling aristocracy and the strategic interests of Great Britain at a time of great international tension. The violent phase of the movement only began after Britain became embroiled in war with revolutionary France. The civil rights movement of 1968 in Northern Ireland was a non-violent agitation, largely of catholics, for social justice, quite independent of nationalism, and the violence in which it soon became involved was started by militant protestants, the counterparts and spiritual descendants of the Orangemen of 1795. The British government, far from being opposed to the civil rights demands, insisted on concessions being made by the government of Northern Ireland, and British military intervention was undertaken to give to catholics the protection that the northern government had failed to provide against protestant attack. The activities of the British army led to the intervention of the I.R.A. in 1970, and from this point onwards the movement for civil rights in Northern Ireland became, for most protestants, inseparable from the Provos' guerilla offensive against Northern Ireland itself. The Provos see themselves as successors of Wolfe Tone and the men of 1916 in a war for national independence, but the image they have acquired in

[2]See his pamphlet *New Ireland: sell-out or opportunity?* ([Belfast], 1972).

protestant eyes is more like that of the Defenders, the catholic counterpart of the Peep O'Day Boys and the Orangemen in Tone's era, or that of the wood-kernes and the tories of the seventeenth century—catholic peasant guerillas who, from the beginning of the plantation, maintained a localised resistance-movement in Ulster against the protestant colonists and the authority of the state. One of the rural areas in which the Provos are strongly entrenched, south County Armagh, was the stronghold of the most famous of Ulster tories, Redmond O'Hanlon.

Just as the rising of 1798 led to the extinction of the Irish parliament and the merging of Ireland politically in the United Kingdom, so the continuing disorder in Northern Ireland has brought about the suspension of the Stormont parliament and the assumption of direct rule by Britain. But there are vital differences between the situations in 1800 and in 1973. Whereas Britain regarded the merger of 1800 as a final settlement of the Irish question, direct rule as introduced in 1972 is intended to be only a temporary expedient, during which a new system of home rule for Northern Ireland can be worked out. And what distinguishes the present Irish crisis from all its predecessors is (a) that Britain has no vital interest in retaining power in Ireland, but on the contrary is committed to a settlement in Northern Ireland on a consensus basis, (b) that twenty-six of Ireland's thirty-two counties are under the sovereignty of a democratically elected parliament, which desires the eventual unification of the whole island, but is vitally interested in promoting a peaceful settlement in Northern Ireland even though this means postponing unification to an indefinite future; and (c) that the elected representatives of the minority in Northern Ireland, the S.D.L.P., are committed to working a new constitution on a basis of partnership and power-sharing with elected representatives of the majority, and of institutional cooperation between Northern Ireland and the Republic. In these new conditions the best hope of a settlement in Northern Ireland would seem to lie.

## Appendix A

# MEMBERS ELECTED TO THE NORTHERN IRELAND ASSEMBLY IN THE GENERAL ELECTION OF 28 JUNE 1973

The party identifications are those used by the candidates at the time of the election. Mrs Dickson, though not technically an official unionist, was returned as a supporter of official unionist policy.

### *Official Unionists*

Agnew, Norman (East Belfast)
Baxter, John Lawson (North Antrim)
Bradford, Roy Hamilton (East Belfast)
Broadhurst, Ronald Joseph Callender (South Down)
Brookeborough, *Viscount* (North Down)
Brownlow, William Steven (North Down)
Campbell, Robert Victor (North Down)
Cardwell, Joshua (East Belfast)
Dickson, Anne Letitia (South Antrim)
Elder, Nelson (South Belfast)
Faulkner, Arthur Brian Deane (South Down)
Hall-Thompson, Robert Lloyd (North Belfast)
Kirk, Herbert Victor (South Belfast)
McCarthy, David[1] (North Antrim)
McIvor, William Basil (South Belfast)
McLachlan, Peter John (South Antrim)
Magee, Reginald Arthur Edward (South Belfast)
Minford, Nathaniel Owens (South Antrim)
Morgan, William James (North Belfast)
Morrell, Leslie James (Londonderry)
Pollock, Thomas Duncan (Mid-Ulster)
Stronge, James Matthew (Armagh)
Whitten, Herbert (Armagh)

### *Alliance Party*

Cooper, Robert George (West Belfast)
Crothers, Derrick Samuel Frederick (South Antrim)

[1]Mr McCarthy was killed in a car accident on 15 July 1973; the vacancy has not yet (Dec. 1973) been filled.

Dunleath, *Baron* (North Down)
Ferguson, John (North Belfast)
Glass, John Basil Caldwell (South Belfast)
McConnell, Robert Dodd (North Down)
Napier, Oliver John (East Belfast)
Wilson, Hugh (North Antrim)

### *Northern Ireland Labour Party*

Bleakley, David Wylie (East Belfast)

### *Unpledged Unionists*

Ardill, Robert Austin (South Antrim)
Conn, Sheena Elizabeth (Londonderry)
Douglas, William Albert Boyd (Londonderry)
Heslip, Herbert James (South Down)
Kilfedder, James Alexander (North Down)
Laird, John Dunn (West Belfast)
Millar, Frank (North Belfast)
Taylor John David (Fermanagh and South Tyrone)
Thompson, William John (Mid-Ulster)
West, Henry William (Fermanagh and South Tyrone)

### *Vanguard Unionist Progressive Party*

Baird, Ernest Austin (Fermanagh and South Tyrone)
Barr, Albert Glenn (Londonderry)
Carson, Thomas Desmond (Armagh)
Craig, William (North Antrim)
Dunlop, John (Mid-Ulster)
Harvey, Cecil (South Down)
Lindsay, John Kennedy (South Antrim)

### *Democratic Unionist Party*

Beattie, William John (South Antrim)
Burns, Thomas Edward (South Belfast)
Craig, James (North Antrim)
Hutchinson, Douglas (Armagh)
McQuade, John (North Belfast)
Paisley, Eileen Emily (East Belfast)
Paisley, Ian Richard Kyle (North Antrim)
Poots, Charles Boucher (North Down)

### *West Belfast Loyalist Coalition*

Coulter, Rose Jean (West Belfast)
Smyth, Hugh (West Belfast)

## *Social Democratic and Labour Party*

Canavan, Michael William Edward (Londonderry)
Cooper, Ivan Averil (Mid-Ulster)
Currie, Joseph Austin (Fermanagh and South Tyrone)
Daly, Thomas Anthony (Fermanagh and South Tyrone)
Devlin, Patrick Joseph (West Belfast)
Duffy, Patrick Aloysius (Mid-Ulster)
Feely, Frank (South Down)
Fitt, Gerard (North Belfast)
Gillespie, Desmond Edward (West Belfast)
Hume, John (Londonderry)
Larkin, Aidan Joseph (Mid-Ulster)
Logue, Hugh Anthony (Londonderry)
McCloskey, Edward Vincent (South Antrim)
McGrady, Edward Kevin (South Down)
Mallon, Seamus (Armagh)
News, Hugh (Armagh)
O'Donoghue, Patrick (South Down)
O'Hagan, John Joseph (North Antrim)
O'Hanlon, Patrick Michael (Armagh)

## Appendix B

## MEMBERS NOMINATED TO THE EXECUTIVE OF NORTHERN IRELAND, NOVEMBER 1973

*Offical Unionists*

### Voting members

Brian Arthur Faulkner (chief executive)
Herbert Victor Kirk (minister of finance)
Roy Hamilton Bradford (minister of the environment)
Leslie James Morrell (minister of agriculture)
William Basil McIvor (minister of education)
John Lawson Baxter (minister of information)

### Non-voting member

Robert Lloyd Hall-Thompson (chief whip)

*Alliance Party*

### Voting member

Oliver John Napier (minister of law reform)

### Non-voting members

John Basil Caldwell Glass (deputy chief-whip)
Robert George Cooper (minister of manpower)

*Social Democratic and Labour Party*

### Voting members

Gerard Fitt (deputy chief-executive)
John Hume (minister of commerce)
Patrick Joseph Devlin (minister of health and social services)
Joseph Austin Currie (minister of local government (housing and planning) )

### Non-voting members

Edward Kevin McGrady (minister of economic planning)
Ivan Averil Cooper (minister of community relations)

## Appendix C

## THE SUNNINGDALE COMMUNIQUÉ, 9 December 1973

(Government Information Services, Dublin:
Government Documentation N.I. 4)

1  The conference between the British and Irish governments and the parties involved in the Northern Ireland executive-designate met at Sunningdale on 6, 7, 8 and 9 December 1973.

2  During the conference, each delegation stated their position on the status of Northern Ireland.

3  The taoiseach said that the basic principle of the conference was that the participants had tried to see what measure of agreement of benefit to all the people concerned could be secured. In doing so, all had reached accommodation with one another on practical arrangements. But none had compromised, and none had asked others to compromise, in relation to basic aspirations. The people of the Republic together with a minority in Northern Ireland, as represented by the S.D.L.P. delegation, continued to uphold the aspiration towards a United Ireland. The only unity they wanted to see was a unity established by consent.

4  Mr Brian Faulkner said that delegates from Northern Ireland came to the conference as representatives of apparently incompatible sets of political aspirations who had found it possible to reach agreement to join together in government because each accepted that in doing so they were not sacrificing principles or aspirations. The desire of the majority of the people of Northern Ireland to remain part of the United Kingdom, as represented by the Unionist and Alliance delegations, remained firm.

5  The Irish government fully accepted and solemnly declared that there could be no change in the status of Northern Ireland until a majority of the people of Northern Ireland desired a change in that status.

The British government solemnly declared that it was, and would remain, its policy to support the wishes of the majority of the people of Northern Ireland. The present status of Northern Ireland is that it is part of the United Kingdom. If in the future, the majority of the people of Northern Ireland should indicate a wish to become part of a United Ireland, the British government would support that wish.

6 The conference agreed that a formal agreement incorporating the declarations of the British and Irish governments would be signed at the formal stage of the conference and registered at the United Nations.

7 The conference agreed that a Council of Ireland would be set up. It would be confined to representatives of the two parts of Ireland, with appropriate safeguards for the British government's financial and other interests. It would comprise a council of ministers with executive and harmonising functions and a consultative role and a consultative assembly with advisory and review functions. The council of ministers would act by unanimity, and would comprise a core of seven members of the Irish government and an equal number of members of the Northern Ireland executive, with provision for the participation of other non-voting members of the Irish government and the Northern Ireland executive or administration when matters within their departmental competence were discussed.

The council of ministers would control the functions of the council. The chairmanship would rotate on an agreed basis between representatives of the Irish Government and of the Northern Ireland executive. Arrangements would be made for the location of the first meeting, and the location of subsequent meetings would be determined by the council of ministers.

The consultative assembly would consist of 60 members, 30 members from Dáil Éireann chosen by the dáil on the basis of proportional representation by the single transferable vote, and 30 members from the Northern Ireland assembly, chosen by that assembly and also on that basis. The members of the consultative assembly would be paid allowances. There would be a secretariat to the council, which would be kept as small as might be commensurate with efficiency in the operation of the council.

The secretariat would service the institutions of the council and would, under the council of ministers, supervise the carrying out of the executive and harmonising functions and the consultative role of the council. The secretariat would be headed by a secretary general.

Following the appointment of a Northern Ireland executive, the Irish government and the Northern Ireland executive would nominate their representatives to a council of ministers. The council of ministers would then appoint a secretary general and decide upon the location of its permanent headquarters. The secretary general would be directed to proceed with the drawing up of plans for such headquarters. The council of Ministers would make arrangements for the recruitment of the staff of the secretariat in a manner and on conditions which would, as far as is practicable, be consistent with those applying to public servants in the two administrations.

8 In the context of its harmonising functions and consultative role, the Council of Ireland would undertake the important

work relating, for instance, to the impact of E.E.C. membership. As for executive functions, the first step would be to define and agree these in details. The conference, therefore, decided that, in view of the administrative complexities involved, studies would at once be set in hand to identify and, prior to the formal stage of the conference, report on areas of common interest in relation to which a Council of Ireland would take executive decisions, and, in appropriate cases, be responsible for carrying those decisions into effect. In carrying out these studies and also in determining what should be done by the council in terms of harmonisation, the objectives to be borne in mind would include the following .

(1) to achieve the best utilisation of scarce skills, expertise and resources;

(2) to avoid in the interests of economy and efficiency, unnecessary duplication of effort; and

(3) to ensure complementary rather than competitive effort where this is to the advantage of agriculture, commerce and industry.

In particular, these studies would be directed to identifying, for the purposes of executive action by the Council of Ireland, suitable aspects of activities in the following broad fields :

(a) exploitation, conservation and development of natural resources and the environment;

(b) agricultural matters (including agricultural research, animal health and operational aspects of the Common Agriculture Policy), forestry and fisheries;

(c) co-operative ventures in the fields of trade and industry;

(d) electricity generation;

(e) tourism;

(f) roads and transport;

(g) advisory services in the field of public health;

(h) sport, culture and the arts.

It would be for the oireachtas and the Northern Ireland assembly to legislate from time to time as to the extent of functions to be devolved to the Council of Ireland. Where necessary, the British government will co-operate in this devolution of functions. Initially the functions to be vested would be those identified in accordance with the procedures set out above and decided, at the formal stage of the conference, to be transferred.

9 (i) During the initial period following the establishment of the council, the revenue of the council would be provided by means of grants from the two administrations in Ireland towards agreed projects and budgets, according to the nature of the service involved.

(ii) It was also agreed that further studies would be put in hand forthwith and completed as soon as possible of methods of financing the council after the initial period which would be consonant with the responsibilities and functions assigned to it.

(iii) It was agreed that the cost of the secretariat of the Council of Ireland would be shared equally, and other services would be financed broadly in proportion to where expenditure or benefit accrues.

(iv) The amount of money required to finance the council's activities will depend upon the functions assigned to it from time to time.

(v) While Britain continues to pay subsidies to Northern Ireland such payments would not involve Britain participating in the council, it being accepted nevertheless that it would be legitimate for Britain to safeguard, in an appropriate way, her financial involvement in Northern Ireland.

10 It was agreed by all parties that persons committing crimes of violence, however motivated, in any part of Ireland should be brought to trial irrespective of the part of Ireland in which they are located. The concern which large sections of the people of Northern Ireland felt about this problem was in particular forcefully expressed by the representatives of the Unionist and Alliance parties. The representatives of the Irish government stated that they understood and fully shared this concern.

Different ways of solving this problem were discussed; among them were the amendment of legislation operating in the two jurisdictions on extradition, the creation of a common law enforcement area in which an all-Ireland court would have jurisdiction, and the extension of the jurisdiction of domestic courts so as to enable them to try offences committed outside the jurisdiction.

It was agreed that problems of considerable legal complexity were involved, and that the British and Irish governments would jointly set up a commission to consider all the proposals put forward at the conference and to recommend, as a matter of extreme urgency, the most effective means of dealing with those who commit these crimes.

The Irish government undertook to take immediate and effective legal steps so that persons coming within their jurisdiction and accused of murder, however motivated, committed in Northern Ireland, will be brought to trial, and it was agreed that any similar reciprocal action that may be needed in Northern Ireland be taken by the appropriate authorities.

11 It was agreed that the council would be invited to consider in what way the principles of the European Convention on Human Rights and Fundamental Freedoms would be expressed in domestic legislation in each part of Ireland. It would recommend whether further legislation or the creation of other institutions, administrative or judicial, is required in either part or embracing the whole island to provide additional

protection in the field of human rights. Such recommendations could include the function of an ombudsman, or commissioner for complaints, or other arrangements of a similar nature which the Council of Ireland might think appropriate.

12 The conference also discussed the question of policing and the need to ensure public support for, and identification with, the police service throughout the whole community. It was agreed that no single set of proposals would achieve these aims overnight, and that time would be necessary. The conference expressed the hope that the wide range of agreement that had been reached, and the consequent formation of a power-sharing executive, would make a major contribution to the creation of an atmosphere throughout the community where there would be widespread support for identification with all the institutions of Northern Ireland.

13 It was broadly accepted that the two parts of Ireland are to a considerable extent interdependent in the whole field of law and order, and that the problems of political violence and identification with the police service cannot be solved without taking account of that fact.

14 Accordingly, the British government stated that, as soon as the security problems were resolved and the new institutions were seen to be working effectively, they would wish to discuss the devolution of responsibility for normal policing, and how this might be achieved with the Northern Ireland executive and the police.

15 With a view to improving policing throughout the island and developing community identification with and support from the police services, the governments concerned will co-operate under the auspices of a Council of Ireland through their respective police authorities. To this end, the Irish government would set up a police authority, appointments to which would be made after consultation with the council of ministers of the Council of Ireland. In the case of the Northern Ireland police authority, appointments would be made after consultation with the Northern Ireland executive, which would consult with the council of ministers of the Council of Ireland. When the two police authorities are constituted, they will make their own arrangements to achieve the objectives set out above.

16 An independent complaints procedure for dealing with complaints against the police will be set up.

17 The secretary of state for Northern Ireland will set up an all-party committee from the assembly to examine how best to introduce effective policing throughout Northern Ireland, with particular reference to the need to achieve public identification with the police.

18 The conference took note of a reaffirmation by the

British government of its firm commitment to bring detention to an end in Northern Ireland for all sections of the community as soon as the security situation permits, and noted also that the secretary of state for Northern Ireland hopes to be able to bring into use his statutory powers of selective release in time for a number of detainees to be released before Christmas.

19 The British government stated that, in the light of the decisions reached at the conference, they would seek the authority of parliament to devolve full powers to the Northern Ireland executive and Northern Ireland assembly as soon as possible. The formal appointment of the Northern Ireland executive would then be made.

20 The conference agreed that a formal conference would be held early in the new year, at which the British and Irish governments and the Northern Ireland executive would meet together to consider reports on the studies which have been commissioned and to sign the agreement reached.

Edward Heath
Liam Mac Cosgair

A. B. D. Faulkner
Gerry Fitt
O. Napier

# SELECT BIBLIOGRAPHY

The following is intended as a guide to further reading on the subject of this book. Some items are included not as scholarship but as documenting the passions, the prejudices and the entrenched attitudes characteristic of Ulster history. Some are included because nothing else is available on their particular subjects. Much of the writing on recent events is inevitably partizan and unsystematic. Of the older books many are, unfortunately, only to be found in specialised or in very large libraries.

## General

George O'Brien. *The four green fields.* Dublin: Talbot Press, 1936.

Hugh Shearman. *Ulster.* London: Hale, 1949 (County Books series).

Hugh Shearman. *Anglo-Irish relations.* London: Faber, 1948.

Nicholas Mansergh. *Britain and Ireland.* London: Longmans, 1942 (Longmans Pamphlets on the British Commonwealth).

Conor Cruise O'Brien. *States of Ireland.* London: Hutchinson, 1972.

J. C. Beckett. *A short history of Ireland.* London: Hutchinson, 5th edition, 1973.

R. Dudley Edwards. *A new history of Ireland.* Dublin: Gill and Macmillan, 1972.

J. C. Beckett. *The making of modern Ireland, 1603-1923.* London: Faber, 1966. Paperback edition, 1969.

P. J. O'Farrell. *Ireland's English question: Anglo-Irish relations, 1534-1970.* London: Batsford, 1970.

F. S. L. Lyons, *Ireland since the famine.* London: Weidenfeld and Nicolson. 1971; revised edition, Fontana, 1973.

Robert Kee. *The green flag: a history of Irish nationalism.* London: Weidenfeld and Nicolson, 1972.

E. E. Evans. *The personality of Ireland.* Cambridge: University Press, 1973.

## Gaelic Ulster

Myles Dillon (ed.). *Early Irish society.* Dublin: Three Candles, 1954 (Thomas Davis Lectures).

Francis J. Byrne. *Irish kings and high kings.* London: Batsford, 1973.

Myles Dillon (ed.). *Irish sagas.* Dublin: Stationery Office, 1959; Cork: Mercier Press, 1968 (Thomas Davis Lectures).

Gerard Murphy. *Saga and myth in ancient Ireland.* Dublin. Three Candles, 1961 (Thomas Davis Lectures).

Rev. George Hill. *An historical account of the MacDonnells of Antrim*. Belfast, 1873.

## The British colony

Cyril Falls. *The birth of Ulster*. London, 1936.

George Hill. *An historical account of the plantation in Ulster . . . 1608-20*. Belfast, 1877. Reprint, Shannon: Irish University Press, 1970.

T. W. Moody. *The Londonderry plantation, 1609-41: the City of London and the plantation in Ulster*. Belfast: Mullan, 1939.

M. P. Maxwell. *The Scottish migration to Ulster in the reign of James I*. London: Routledge and Kegan Paul, 1973.

J. B. Woodburn. *The Ulster Scot, his history and religion*. London, 1915.

M. P. Maxwell. 'Strafford, the Ulster-Scots nd the convenanters' in *Irish Historical Studies*, xviii, no. 72 (Sept. 1973), pp 524-51.

J. G. Simms. *Jacobite Ireland, 1685-91*. London: Routledge and Kegan Paul, 1969.

J. G. Simms. *The siege of Derry*. Dublin: A.P.C.K., 1966.

## The eighteenth century

W. E. H. Lecky. *History of Ireland in the eighteenth century*. 5 vols. London, 1892.

J. C. Beckett. *Protestant dissent in Ireland, 1687-1780*. London, 1948.

R. J. Dickson. *Ulster emigration to colonial America, 1718-75*. London, 1966.

Frank MacDermot. *Theobald Wolfe Tone*. London: Macmillan, 1939; revised edition, Tralee: Anvil Books, 1968.

H. M. Hyde. *The rise of Castlereagh*. London, 1933.

D. A. Chart (ed.). *The Drennan letters*. Belfast: H.M.S.O., 1931.

Hereward Senior. *Orangeism in Ireland and Britain, 1795-1836*. London: Routledge and Kegan Paul, 1966.

## The union, 1801-1921

Oliver MacDonagh. *Ireland*. Englewood Cliffs, New Jersey: Prentice-Hall, 1968.

G. Locker Lampson. *A consideration of the state of Ireland in the nineteenth century*. London, 1907.

Gearóid Ó Tuathaigh. *Ireland before the famine, 1798-1848*. Dublin: Gill and Macmillan, 1972 (The Gill History of Ireland, ed. J. F. Lydon and Margaret MacCurtain).

L. M. Cullen (ed.). *The formation of the Irish economy*. Cork: Mercier Press, 1968 (Thomas Davis Lectures).

T. W. Moody and J. C. Beckett (ed.). *Ulster since 1800*. 2

series: (1) *A political and economic survey;* (2) *A social survey,* London: B.B.C., 1955, 1957.

H. S. Morrison. *Modern Ulster: its character, customs, politics and industries.* London, 1920.

Hereward Senior. *Orangeism in Ireland and Britain, 1795-1836.* London: Routledge and Kegan Paul, 1966.

Nicholas Mansergh. *The Irish question, 1840-1921.* London: Allen and Unwin, 1965.

Joseph Lee. *The modernisation of Irish society, 1848-1918.* Dublin: Gill and Macmillan, 1973 (The Gill History of Ireland, ed. J. F. Lydon and Margaret MacCurtain).

Patrick Buckland. *Irish unionism.* Vol. i: *The Anglo-Irish and the new Ireland, 1885-1922.* Dublin: Gill and Macmillan, 1972.

Patrick Buckland. *Irish unionism.* Vol. ii: *Ulster unionism and the origins of Northern Ireland, 1886-1922.* Dublin: Gill and Macmillan, 1972.

Patrick Buckland (ed.). *Irish unionism: a documentary history.* Belfast: H.M.S.O., 1973.

J. F. Harbinson. *The Ulster unionist party, 1882-1973:* its *development and organisation.* Belfast: Blackstaff Press, 1973.

C. Gavan Duffy. *Young Ireland: a fragment of Irish history, 1840-45.* London, 1880. Final revision, 2 vols, London, 1896.

C. Gavan Duffy. *The league of north and south: an episode in Irish history, 1850-1854.* London, 1886.

Thomas MacKnight, *Ulster as it is, or twenty-eight years' experience as an Irish editor.* 2 vols. London, 1890.

W. S. Armour *Armour of Ballymoney.* London, 1934.

C. Cruise O'Brien (ed.). *The shaping of modern Ireland.* London: Routledge and Kegan Paul, 1960 (Thomas Davis Lectures). (Includes essays on Sir Edward Carson by R. B. McDowell and on W. J. Pirrie by R. D. C. Black.)

Breandán Mac Giolla Choille (ed.). *Intelligence notes, 1913-16, preserved in the State Paper Office.* Dublin: S.O., 1966.

F. X. Martin (ed.). *Leaders and men of the Easter rising: Dublin 1916.* London: Methuen, 1967.

K. B. Nowlan (ed.). *The making of 1916: studies in the history of the rising.* Dublin: S.O., 1969.

*Partition*

Ronald McNeill. *Ulster's stand for union.* London, 1922.

F. H. Crawford. *Guns for Ulster.* London, 1947.

Denis Gwynn. *The history of partition, 1912-25.* Dublin, 1950.

Francis W. O'Brien. (ed.). *Divided Ireland: the roots of the conflict.* Rochford, Illinois, 1971.

Thomas E. Hachey (ed.). *The problem of partition: peril to world peace.* Chicago: Rand McNally, 1972.

H. M. Hyde. *The life of Lord Carson.* London, 1953.

Edward Majoribanks and Ian Colvin. *Life of Lord Carson.* 2 vols, London, 1932, 1934.

114

Patrick Buckland. *Irish unionism*. Vol. ii: *Ulster unionism and the origins of Northern Ireland, 1886-1922*. Dublin: Gill and Macmillan, 1973.

A. T. Q. Stewart. *The Ulster crisis*. London: Faber, 1967.

D. G. Boyce. 'British conservative opinion, the Ulster question and the partition of Ireland, 1912-21' in *Irish Historical Studies*, xvii, no. 65 (Mar. 1970), pp 89-112.

T. D. Williams (ed.). *The Irish struggle*, 1916-26. London: Routledge and Kegan Paul, 1966 (Thomas Davis Lectures).

Thomas Jones. *Whitehall diary*. Vol. iii: *Ireland, 1918-25*. London: Oxford University Press, 1971.

*Official report, debate on the treaty between Great Britain and Ireland signed in London on the 6th December 1921*. Dublin: Stationery Office.

*Dáil Éireann, private sessions of second dáil, 1921-2*. Dublin: Stationery Office.

*Report of the Irish boundary commission 1925*. Introduction by Geoffrey J. Hand. Shannon: Irish University Press, 1969.

M. W. Heslinga. *The Irish border as a cultural divide: a contribution to the study of regionalism in the British Isles*. Assen: Van Gorcum, 1971.

Benedict Kiely. *Counties of contention: a study of the origins and implications of the partition of Ireland*. Cork, 1945.

## Ireland, 1921-73

Oliver MacDonagh. *Ireland*. Englewood Cliffs, New Jersey: Prentice Hall, 1968.

T. D. Williams (ed.). *The Irish struggle, 1916-26*. London: Routledge and Kegan Paul, 1966 (Thomas Davis Lectures).

Francis MacManus (ed.). *The years of the great test, 1926-39*. Cork: Mercier Press, 1957 (Thomas Davis Lectures).

K. B. Nowlan and T. D. Williams (ed.). *Ireland in the war years and after, 1939-51*. Dublin: Gill and Macmillan, 1969 (Thomas Davis Lectures).

T. P. Coogan. *Ireland since the rising*. London, 1966.

T. P. Coogan. *The I.R.A.* London: Pall Mall Press, 1970.

J. Bowyer Bell. *The secret army: a history of the I.R.A., 1915-1970* London: Anthony Blond, 1970.

Nicholas Mansergh. *The Irish Free State: its government and politics*. London 1934.

Basil Chubb. *The government and politics of Ireland*. London: Oxford University Press, 1970.

J. H. Whyte. *Church and state in modern Ireland, 1923-1970*. Dublin: Gill and Macmillan, 1971.

## Northern Ireland

D. A. Chart. *A history of Northern Ireland*. Belfast, [1922].

Hugh Shearman. *Not an inch: a study of Northern Ireland and Lord Craigavon*. London, 1942.

Hugh Shearman. *Northern Ireland, 1921-1971*. Belfast: H.M.S.O., 1971.

J. C. Beckett. 'Northern Ireland' in *Journal of Contemporary History*, vi (1971), pp 121-34.

St John Ervine. *Craigavon, Ulsterman*. London, 1949.

John W. Blake. *Northern Ireland in the second world war*. Belfast: H.M.S.O., 1956.

Nicholas Mansergh. *The government of Northern Ireland*. London, 1936.

*Report of a commission of inquiry appointed to examine the purpose and effect of the Civil Authorities (Special Powers) Acts (Northern Ireland) 1922 & 1935*. London: National Council for Civil Liberties, 1936.

D. G. Neill (ed.). *Devolution of government: the experiment in Northern Ireland*. London, 1953.

Thomas Wilson (ed.). *Ulster under home rule: a study of the political and economic problems of Northern Ireland*. London, 1955.

Hugh Shearman. *How Northern Ireland is governed*. Belfast, 1963.

R. J. Lawrence. *The government of Northern Ireland: public finance and public services, 1921-64*. Oxford: Clarendon Press, 1965.

J. F. Harbinson. *The Ulster unionist party, 1882-1973: its development and organisation*. Belfast: Blackstaff Press, 1973.

Arthur Hezlett, *The 'B Specials': a history of the Ulster Special Constabulary*. London: Pan Books, 1972.

Denis P. Barritt and Charles F. Carter. *The Northern Ireland problem: a study in group relations*. London: Oxford University Press, 1962. Second edition, 1972.

*The Ulster year book*. Belfast: Ministry of Finance, 1926-.

Richard Rose. *Governing without consensus: an Irish perspective*. London: Faber, 1971.

### Belfast

J. C. Beckett and R. E. Glasscock. *Belfast: the origin and growth of an industrial city*. London, B.B.C., 1967.

Mary McNeill. *The life and times of Mary Ann McCracken, 1770-1866: a Belfast panorama*. Dublin: Allen Figgis, 1960.

Andrew Boyd. *Holy war in Belfast*. Tralee: Anvil Books, 1969.

Ian Budge and Cornelius O'Leary. *Belfast, approach to crisis: a study of Belfast politics, 1603-1970*. London: Macmillan, 1973.

### Orangeism

Hereward Senior. *Orangeism in Ireland and Britain, 1795-1836*. London: Routledge and Kegan Paul, 1966.

R. M. Sibbett. *Orangeism in Ireland and throughout the*

116

*empire*. 1st ed., Belfast, 1913; revised and enlarged edition, London, 1939.

M. W. Dewar, John Brown and S. E. Long. *Orangeism: a new historical appreciation*. Belfast: T. H. Jordan, 1967.

Tony Gray. *The Orange Order*. London: Bodley Head, 1972.

J. W. Boyle. 'The Belfast Protestant Association and the Independent Orange Order, 1901-10' in *Irish Historical Studies*, xiv, no. 50 (Sept. 1962), pp 117-52.


*Economic and social life*

K. E. Isles and N. Cuthbert. *An economic survey of Northern Ireland*. Belfast, 1957.

Conrad Gill. *The rise of the Irish linen industry*. Oxford: Clarendon Press, 1925; reprinted, 1964.

E. R. R. Green. *The Lagan valley: a local history of the industrial revolution*. London: Faber, 1949.

E. R. R. Green. *The industrial archaeology of County Down*. Belfast, 1963.

W. A. McCutcheon. *The canals of the north of Ireland*. London, 1965.

H. D. Gribbon. *The history of water power in Ulster*. Newton Abbot: David and Charles, 1969.

W. E. Coe, *The engineering industry of the north of Ireland*. Newton Abbot: David and Charles, 1969.

W. A. Maguire. *The Downshire estates in Ireland, 1801-1845*. Oxford: Clarendon Press, 1972.

John Hamilton. *Sixty years' experience as an Irish landlord*. London: 1894.

E. Estyn Evans. *Irish heritage: the landscape, the people, and their work*. Dundalk: Tempest, 1942.

Gilbert Camblin. *The town in Ulster*. Belfast: Mullan, 1951.

Robert Lynd. *Home life in Ireland*. London, 1909.

Lynn Doyle. *An Ulster childhood*. 1901.

E. Estyn Evans. *Mourne country*. Dundalk: Tempest, 1967.

J. M. Mogey. *Rural life in Northern Ireland: five regional studies*. London: Oxford University Press, 1937.

Rosemary Harris. *Prejudice and tolerance in Ulster: a study in neighbours and 'strangers' in a border community*. Manchester: University Press; Totowa (N.J.): Rowman & Littlefield, 1972.


*Religion and education*

J. S. Reid. *History of the presbyterian church in Ireland*. Edited by W. D. Killen. 3 vols. Belfast, 1867.

William Gibson. *The year of grace: a history of the Ulster revival of 1859*. Edinburgh, 1860; jubilee ed., Edinburgh and London, 1909.

Isaac Nelson. *The year of delusion: a review of 'The year of grace'*. Belfast, 1850.

117

W. D. Killen. *Reminiscences of a long life.* London, 1901.

W. A. Phillips (ed.). *History of the Church of Ireland,* Vol. iii. Oxford: Clarendon Press, 1932.

C. F. D'Arcy. *The adventures of a bishop: a phase of Irish life: a personal and historical narrative.* London, 1934.

J. F. MacNeice. *Carrickfergus and its contacts: some chapters in the history of Ulster.* Carrickfergus, 1928.

J. F. MacNeice. *The Church of Ireland in Belfast. 1778-1931.* 1931.

R. P. McDermott and D. A. Webb. *Irish protestantism today. and tomorrow: a demographic study.* Dublin and Belfast: A.P.C.K., [1945].

Michael Hurley (ed.). *Irish anglicanism, 1869-1969.* Dublin: Allen Figgis, 1970.

James MacCaffrey. *History of the catholic church in the nineteenth century, 1789-1908.* 2 vols. Dublin, 1909.

George Crolly. *Life of the Most Reverend Doctor Crolly, archbishop of Armagh.* Dublin, 1851.

James MacDevitt. *The Most Reverend James McDevitt. D. D., bishop of Raphoe: a memoir.* Dublin, 1880.

R. B. O'Brien. *The life of Lord Russell of Killowen.* London, 1901.

D. M. Akenson. *The Irish educational experiment: the national system of education in the nineteenth century.* London: Routledge and Kegan Paul, 1970.

D. M. Akenson. *Education and enmity: the control of schooling in Northern Ireland, 1920-1950.* Newton Abbot: David and Charles, 1973.

John Jamieson. *The history of the Royal Belfast Academical Institution, 1810-1960.* Belfast: Mullan, 1959.

David Kennedy. *Towards a university: an account of some institutions for higher education in Ireland and elsewhere, and of the attitude of Irish catholics to them, with particular reference to Queen's College and Queen's University, Belfast.* Belfast, [1946].

T. W. Moody and J. C. Beckett. *Queen's, Belfast, 1849-1949: the history of a university.* 2 vols. London: Faber, 1959.

Robert Allen. *The Presbyterian College, Belfast, 1853-1953.* Belfast, 1954.

Finlay Holmes. *Magee, 1865-1965: the evolution of the Magee colleges.* Belfast, [1965].

*Higher education in Northern Ireland: report of the committee appointed by the minister of finance* (27 November 1964). Cmd 475 (N.I.). Belfast: H.M.S.O., 1965 (The Lockwood report).

*The present situation, 1968-73*

Richard Rose. *Governing without consensus: an Irish perspective.* London: Faber, 1971.

Denis P. Barritt and Arthur Booth. *Orange and Green: a*

*quaker study of community relations in Northern Ireland.* Sedbergh, Yorks: Northern Friends Peace Board, 1967; revised edition, 1970, 1972.

Liam de Paor. *Divided Ulster.* London: Penguin Books, 1970.

Owen Dudley Edwards. *The sins of our fathers: roots of conflict in Northern Ireland.* Dublin: Gill and Macmillan, 1970.

*The Ulster debate: report of a study group of the Institute for the Study of Conflict.* London: Bodley Head, 1972. (Papers by J. C. Beckett, Sir Frederick Catherwood, Lord Chalfont, Garret FitzGerald, F. S. L. Lyons).

*Administration: Journal of the Institute of Public Administration of Ireland,* vol. xx, no. 4, 1972 (a special issue on the theme 'The Irish Dimension').

Ian Budge and Cornelius O'Leary. *Belfast, approach to crisis: a study of Belfast politics, 1603-1970.* London: Macmillan, 1973.

Michael McInerney. *Trade unions bid for peace in north.* Dublin: *Irish Times,* 1970. (Four articles reprinted from the *Irish Times,* Dec. 1969-Jan. 1970).

Charles McCarthy. 'Civil strife and the growth of trade union unity: the case of Ireland' in *Government and Opposition,* viii, no. 4 (autumn 1973).

Morris Fraser. *Children in conflict: an intimate portrait of the casualties of violence.* London: Secker and Warburg, 1973.

Martin Wallace. *Drums and guns: revolution in Ulster.* Dublin and London: Geoffrey Chapman, 1970.

Patrick Riddell. *Fire over Ulster.* London: Hamish Hamilton, 1970.

T. P. Coogan. *The I.R.A.* London: Pall Mall Press, 1970.

J. Bowyer Bell. *The secret army: a history of the I.R.A., 1915-1970.* London: Anthony Blond, 1970; Sphere Books edition, 1972.

Bowes Egan and Vincent McCormack. *Burntollet.* London: L.R.S. Publications, 1969.

Clive Limpkin. *The battle of Bogside.* London: Penguin Books, 1972.

Sunday Times Insight team. *Ulster.* London: Penguin Books, 1972.

John McGuffin. *Internment.* Tralee: Anvil Books, 1973.

David Boulton. *The U.V.F., 1966-73: an anatomy of loyalist rebellion.* Dublin: Torc Books, 1973.

Martin Dillon and Denis Lehane. *Political murder in Northern Ireland.* London: Penguin Books, 1973.

Patrick Marrinan. *Paisley: man of wrath.* Tralee: Anvil Book 1973.

Terence O'Neill (Lord O'Neill). *Ulster at the crossroads.* London: Faber, 1970.

Terence O'Neill (Lord O'Neill). *The autobiography of Terence O'Neill, prime minister of Northern Ireland, 1963-9.* London: Rupert Hart-Davis, 1972.

119

Harold Wilson. *The labour government, 1964-70*. London: Weidenfeld and Nicolson, and Michael Joseph, 1971.

James Callaghan. *A house divided: the dilemma of Northern Ireland*. London: Collins, 1973.

John Lynch. *Speeches and statements: Irish unity, Northern Ireland, Anglo-Irish relations, August 1969-October 1971*. Dublin: Government Information Bureau, 1971.

Bernadette Devlin. *The price of my soul*. London: Pan Books, 1969.

David Bleakley. *Peace in Ulster*. London. Mowbrays, 1972.

Garret FitzGerald. *Towards a new Ireland*. London: Charles Knight, 1972.

J. D. A. Robb. *New Ireland: sell-out or opportunity?* [Belfast, 1972.].

[Rosamund Mitchell.] *One island, two nations*. [Dublin]: Worker's Association for a Democratic Settlement of the National Conflict in Ireland, 1973.

Padraig Ó Snodaigh. *Hidden Ulster (the other hidden Ireland)*. Dublin: Clodhanna Teo, 1973.

The Provisional I.R.A. *Freedom struggle*. [Dublin], 1973.

The Presbyterian Church in Ireland. *The Northern Ireland situation: a selection of church statements*. No. 1 (1968-72), no. 2 (1972-3). Belfast, 1972, 1973.

Cahal B. Daly. *Violence in Ireland and Christian conscience: from addresses given by Cahal B. Daly, bishop of Ardagh and Clonmacnois*. Dublin: Veritas Publications, 1973.

'The Irish conflict and Christian conscience' in *The Furrow*, Sept. 1973, pp 554-80 (a report by Pro Mundi Vita, the international research and information centre, Brussels, to decision-makers in the catholic church).

### New Ulster Movement publications
(Published by the New Ulster Movement, 3 Botanic Avenue, Belfast)

1  *The reform of Stormont* (June 1971).
2  *A commentary on the programme of reforms for Northern Ireland* (June 1971).
3  *Northern Ireland: the way forward* (Nov. 1971).
4  *Northern Ireland and the common market* (Jan. 1972).
5  *Two Irelands or one?* (May 1972).
6  *Violence and Northern Ireland* (June 1972).
7  *A new constitution for Northern Ireland* (Aug. 1972).
8  *Ireland—towards the return of the rule of law* (Dec. 1972).
9  *Tribalism or Christianity in Ireland?* (Sept. 1973).

### Government reports and papers

*Disturbances in Northern Ireland: report of the commission appointed by the governor of Northern Ireland* (16 August

1969). Cmd 532 (N.I.). Belfast: H.M.S.O., 1969. (The Cameron report)

*A commentary by the government of Northern Ireland to accompany the Cameron report* (September 1969) Cmd 534 (N.I.). Belfast: H.M.S.O., 1969.

*Report of the advisory committee on police in Northern Ireland* (3 October 1969). Cmd 535 (N.I.). Belfast: H.M.S.O., 1969. (The Hunt report)

*Review body on local government in Northern Ireland 1970, chairman Patrick A. Macrory Esq., report* (29 May 1970). Cmd 546 (N.I.). Belfast: H.M.S.O., 1970. (The Macrory report)

*A record of constructive change* (August 1971). Cmd 598 (N.I.).

*Report of the enquiry into allegations against the security forces of physical brutality in Northern Ireland arising out of events on the 9th August 1971* (3 November 1971). Cmd 4823. London: H.M.S.O., 1971. (The Compton report)

*Report of the committee of privy counsellors appointed to consider unauthorised procedures for the interrogation of persons suspected of terrorism* (31 January 1972). Cmnd 4901. London: H.M.S.O., 1972. (The Parker report)

*Violence and civil disturbances in Northern Ireland in 1969: report of tribunal of inquiry* (4 February 1972). Cmd 566 (N.I.). 2 vols. Belfast: H.M.S.O., 1972 (The Scarman report)

*Report of the tribunal appointed to inquire into the events on Sunday, 30th January, 1972, which led to loss of life in connection with the procession in Londonderry on that day* by the Rt. Hon. Lord Widgery (10 April 1972). London: H.M.S.O., 1972. (The Widgery report)

*The future of Northern Ireland: a paper for discussion* (October 1972). London: H.M.S.O., 1972. (Mr Whitelaw's green paper)

*Report of the commission to consider legal procedures to deal with terrorist activities in Northern Ireland* (December 1972). Cmnd 5185. London: H.M.S.O., 1972 (The Diplock report)

*Northern Ireland constitutional proposals* (March 1973). Cmnd 5259. London: H.M.S.O., 1973. (Mr Whitelaw's white paper)

*Records and works of reference*

*The annual register*

*Who's who*

*Who's who, what's what and where in Ireland.* In association with the *Irish Times.* London and Dublin: Geoffrey Chapman, 1973.

*The Ulster year book.* Belfast: Ministry of Finance, 1926- .

Sydney Elliott. *Northern Ireland parliamentary election results, 1921-1972.* Chichester: Political Reference Publications, 1973.

James Knight and Nicholas Baxter-Moore (ed.). *Northern Ireland local government elections, 30 May 1973*: results for each district electoral area arranged in party order. London: The Arthur McDonnell Fund, 1973.

Richard Deutsch and Vivien Magowan. *Northern Ireland, 1968-73: a chronology of events*. Vol. i: 1968-71. Belfast: Blackstaff Press, 1971.

*Hansard's parliamentary debates, third series*. Vols i-ccclvi (1830-91). London, 1831-91. (This is continued by the two following series.)

*The parliamentary debates (authorised edition), fourth series*. Vols i-cxcix (1892-1908). London, 1892-[1909].

*The parliamentary debates (official report), 5th series, house of commons*. Vol. i- 1969- ). London: H.M.S.O., [1909]- .

*The public general acts passed in the thirty-third and thirty-fourth years of . . . Queen Victoria . . .* [etc]. London: Eyre and Spottiswoode, 1870-86; H.M.S.O., 1887- .

*The parliamentary debates, official report, 1st series, . . . Northern Ireland*. Vol i- , 1921- . Belfast: H.M.S.O., 1921- .

*The public general acts of 1921 passed in the twelfth year of King George the fifth, being the first session of the first parliament of Northern Ireland* [etc.]. Belfast: H.M.S.O., 1922- .

*Statutory rules and orders of Northern Ireland, 1923* [etc.]. Belfast: H.M.S.O., 1925- .

*Dáil Éireann, miontuairisc an chead dala, 1919-1921 (minutes of the proceedings of the first parliament of the republic of Ireland, 1919-1921)*, official record. Dublin: S.O.

*Iris Dháil Éireann, tuairsg oifigiúil, diosboireacht ar an gconnradh dir Éire agus Sasana do signigheadh i Iundain ar an badh lá de mhí na Nodlag 1921 (official report, debate on the treaty between Great Britain and Ireland signed in London on the 6th December 1921)*. Dublin: S.O.

*Dáil Éireann, suíonna príobháideacha an dara dáil . . . (private sessions of second dáil, 1921-2)*. Dublin: S.O., [1973].

*Dáil Éireann, tuairisg oifigiúil (official report) . . . 1921-2*. Dublin: S.O.

*Dáil Éireann . . . , disbóireachtaí párliminte (parliamentary debates), tuairsg oifigiúil (official report)*. Vol. i- , 1922- . Dublin: S.O.

*The Constitution of the Irish Free State (Saorstát Éireann) Act 1922, and the public general acts passed by the Oireachtas of Saorstát Éireann during the year 1922*. (This is continued by the two following series.)

*The public general acts passed by the Oireachtas of Saorstát Éireann during the year 1923* [etc.]. Dublin: S.O.

*The acts of the Oireachtas passed in the year 1938* [etc.]. Dublin: S.O.

F. B. Chubb (ed.). *A source book of Irish government*. Dublin: Institute of Public Administration, 1964.

*Minutes of the General Assembly of the Presbyterian Church in Ireland, 1840* [etc.]. Belfast, 1840- .
*General Assembly of the Presbyterian Church in Ireland, annual reports.*

*Annual Reports of the Irish Trade Union Congress.*

*Annual Reports of the Irish Congress of Trade Unions.*

### Newspapers

The main source of information about recent events is, of course, the newspapers, of which the following are specially useful. There is an extensive list in J. Bowyer Bell, *The secret army* (Sphere Books, 1972), pp 454-7.

Belfast

*Belfast News Letter* (unionist)
*Belfast Telegraph* (liberal unionist)
*Irish News* (nationalist)
*Ulster Protestant* (Paisleyite)
*Protestant Telegraph* (Paisleyite)
*Fortnight*

Dublin

*Irish Independent*
*Irish Press*
*Irish Times* (independent)
*United Irishman* (1948- ; Sinn Féin)
*An Phoblacht* (1970- ; Sinn Féin (Kevin Street)
*Hibernia*: *fortnightly review.*

London

*The Daily Telegraph*
*The Times*
*The Guardian*
*The Observer*
*The Sunday Times*

# INDEX

In twentieth-century dates, only the third and fourth figures as a rule are given.

British government and N.I.: 34, 38-9, 48-9; decision to intervene in (Aug. 69), 48; sends troops to, 48-50; introduces direct rule in (Mar. 72), 50; provides new constitution for (73), 50-53, 56-7; and Sunningdale agreement, vii-viii, 106-11

Brookeborough, Lord, 32

Bunting, Major Ronald, 60

Burntollet, 35-6, 60

Butt, Isaac, 21

Caledon, 32

Callaghan, James, 48-9, 50

Cameron report, 26, 30, 33, 35-6, 60-61, 119-20

Cameron, Lord, 26

Campbell, James, 26

Carrickfergus, 3, 40

Carson, Sir Edward, 23

Carter, Charles F., 26

Catholic church: proscribed 3; and relief measures, 10-11; and the union, 13; restored, 14; protestant fears of, 14, 23, 26, 46, 59-60, 62; and the national schools, 17; and university education, 17; and Queen's University, Belfast, 18-19; defied by I.R.B., 21; and by I.R.A., 70, 83-4; joins with protestant churches in condemning violence, 83-4: and Dundalk conference, 84

Catholic emancipation, 10-11, 14

Catholic relief aid (1793), 11

Catholics in Ulster: before 1603, 3; in the 17th century, 4, 8-9; in the 18th century, 10-13; in the 19th century, 14, 19-22; grievances of, in N.I., 26-32; their identification with nationalism, 14. 19-22, 43: and the constitution of N.I., 27; and the I.R.A., 27, 29. 46, 49-50, 65-7, 70, 75, 76-7, 83-4; and the British army, 49-50, 67, 68,

90; geographical distribution of, 69; and the S.D.L.P., 76-7; and the Alliance Party, 78

Cavan; county of, 5, 6, 22, 25

Cease-fire : by Officials (29 May, 72), 72; by Provos (26 June 72), 68

Chequers meeting (Sept. 71), 91-2

Chichester-Clark, James, 37, 38-41, 61

Children and violence in N.I., 68

Christianity, conversion of Ireland to, 2

Church of Ireland : 80; established by law, 3; in 17th century Ulster, 7, 9; and protestant ascendancy, 10; and presbyterians, 10, 14; and primary education, 17; and higher education, 17-18; and Queen's College, Belfast, 18, 19; disestablishment of, 16, 98; condemnation of violence, 83-4; and Dundalk conference, 84

Churches, peace-efforts of, 70, 80-84

Churchill, Winston, 22-3

Civil Liberties, National Council for (G. B.), 29

Civil Rights Association (N.I.), 30, 33-4

Civil rights movement, 33-6, 37-8, 65. 72, 73, 94

Civil war (22-3), 24

Clann Aedha Bhuidhe, 3

Clergy, cooperation among, in condemning violence, 83-4

Coalisland, 32

Coleraine, 3, 31, 41

Colonial nationalism in Ulster, 10, 14

Compton report, 67, 120

Community relations commission, 39

Community relations, ministry of, 39

Complaints, commissioner for 38

and higher education, 17, 18; attitude to protestant-catholic relations, 80-81; and to present violence, 82-3

Presbyterians in Ulster: in the 17th century, 7-9; in the 18th century, 10-11; in the 19th century, 14; in the 20th century, 80-83

Primary education, 16, 17-18, 25

Proportional representation, 27, 52, 53, 78

Protection rackets, 74, 94

Protestant ascendancy: in the 18th century, 10, 12; in the 19th century, 14, 20; in the 20th century, 27, 57, 65, 72, 94, 97, 98-9

'Protestant backlash', 58, 65, 72-5

Protestant dissenters, 8, 10, 11

Protestant para-military organisations, 58, 72, 74, 75

Protestant radicalism, 11, 97

Protestants in Ulster: in the 17th century, 4, 7, 8-9; in the 18th century, 10-13; in the 19th century, 14-20, 23; their identification with unionism, 14, 20, 23, 26-7; their historic role, 96-7; resistence to British authority, 97

Provisional I.R.A.: origin of (Dec. 69), 65-6; guerilla campaign of, 66-7, 68-9; and local government elections, 54; truce with Whitelaw (June 73), 68; their peace plan, 68; their conception of themselves, 69-71, 100-01; their political theory. 70, 71; their attitude to other nationalists and reforming unionists, 71; to Craig, 71; to Officials, 71-2

Provos, see Provisional I.R.A.

Public prosecutors, 39

Queen's College, Belfast, 18-19

Queen's Colleges, 16, 18

Queen's University, Belfast, 18-19, 35, 99

R.T.E., see Radio Telefís Eireann

R.U.C., see Royal Ulster Constabulary

Radio Telefís Eireann, 34, 89, 95

Railway building, 15

Reconciliation, efforts for, in N.I., 79-89

Redmond John, 23

Referendums: (in Irish Republic) on E.E.C. (10 May 72), 91; on catholic church (7 Dec. 72), 91; (in N.I.), on border (3 Mar. 73), 53, 92-3

Reform programme of N.I. government, 33-4, 37-42

Republican Clubs, 54, 72

'Right to live', 88

Robb, John D.A., 100

Roman Catholic Church see catholic church

Royal Belfast Academical Institution, 17

Royal Irish Constabulary, 16

Royal Ulster Constabulary: 27-8; and civil rights marches (68-9), 33-6; misconduct of, 35-6, 67, 90; unable to control violence, Aug. 69, 37; and British intervention, 48-9, 52; reform of, 38-9, 42, 49; 73, 77

S.D.A., see Shankill Defence Association

S.D.L.P., see Social Democratic and Labour Party

Scarman report, 37 n. 6, 48 n. 1, 120

Scott, Sandy, 87, 88-9

Scots in Ulster, 3, 5, 7-9, 11

Secretary of state for N.I., 50, 53

Sectarian assassinations, 64, 73, 74

Segregated Education, 18, 81

Shankill Defence Association, 73

guard 74; embroiled with British army, 75
Ulster Defence Regiment, 39
Ulster Freedom Fighters, 75
Ulster plantation, 5-7
Ulster Protestant Volunteers, 60
Ulster Scots, *see* Scots in Ulster
Ulster Special Constabulary: 27-8; and British intervention, 48-9; misconduct of, 27, 35; disbandment of, 33, 39, 49, 73; in Ulster Vanguard, 58
Ulster Unionist Council, 57-8
Ulster Unionist Party: character of, 27; commitment to reform (Feb. 69), 37-8; disintegration of, 54-6, 57-65; 50
Ulster unionists, *see* Unionists
Ulster Vanguard, 58-9, 62-3
Ulster Volunteer Force: (1913) 23; (1966) 28, 30, 64, 65, 72-3, 74, 77
Union of G.B. and Ireland: origin of, 12-13; Ulster protestant support for, 14-15; benefits of, 16-19, 43
Unionists: (1801-1921) 14-15, 19, 20, 22-4; (21-73) 26-7, 36-7, 42, 43, 53-6, 97; disintegration among, 57-65; working-class disillusionment among, 63-5; their sense of being abandoned by Britain, 65; *and see* Loyalists
United Irishmen, 11-12, 14, 97, 100
Unpledged unionists, 54, 55-6, 65, 102

V.U.P.P., *see* Vanguard

Unionist Progressive Party
Vanguard Unionist Progressive Party: formation of (Nov. 72) 63; in assembly elections (73), 54, 56, 102
Voluntary organisations, and violence in N.I., 95-6.

Ward, Peter, 73
Wentworth, Thomas, earl of Strafford, 8
West, Rt Hon. Harry, 56, 102
West Belfast Loyalist Coalition, 54, 56, 102
Whiteboys, 12
Whitelaw, William: secretary of state for N.I., 50; convenes conference at Darlington, 50; his green paper (Oct. 72), 51-2, 91, 92, 120; his white paper, 52-3, 120; and new deal for N.I., 53, 56-7; truce with Provos (June 72), 68; meeting with Provos (7 July 72), 68; and 'operation Motorman', 68; Craig and Paisley hostile to his assembly plan, 63; and Jack Lynch, 88, 92; resignation of (3 Dec. 73), viii
Widgery report, 120
William III, prince of Orange, 96
Wilson, Harold, 48-50, 62
Wilson, Thomas, 40
Wood-kernes, 6, 101
Workers' Committee for the Defence of the Constitution, 63
Working-classes and sectarian conflict, 19-20, 61-2, 63-5, 71-5, 85-9
World War I, 22-3, 24
World War II, 45